Dear Dad

Merry Christmas! '92

love Robyn
+ Brian

STEAM TRAINS
A WORLD PORTRAIT

All photographs taken by Colin Garratt exclusively on Agfachrome film

MALLARD PRESS
An imprint of BDD Promotional Book Company, Inc.
666 Fifth Avenue, New York, N.Y. 10103

Mallard Press and its accompanying design and logo
are trademarks of BDD Promotional Book Company, Inc.

CLB 2331
© 1989 Colour Library Books Ltd., Godalming, Surrey, England.
© 1989 Illustrations: Colin Garratt, Newton Harcourt, Leicestershire, England.
Published in the United States of America in 1989 by The Mallard Press.
Color separation by Hong Kong Graphic Arts Ltd., Hong Kong.
Printed by Leefung Asco Printers Ltd., Hong Kong.
All rights reserved.
ISBN 0 792 45168 6

STEAM TRAINS
A WORLD PORTRAIT

Colin Garratt

MALLARD PRESS

Contents

STEAM TRAINS
A WORLD PORTRAIT

It is popularly supposed that the world's first steam locomotive was Stephenson's *Rocket*. In truth, however, the first example appeared exactly a quarter of a century before this in 1804, when Richard Trevithick's engine emerged from a South Wales ironworks. Yet it was with the *Rocket* that certain basic principles were established: it had a multi-flue tube boiler, used exhaust steam to create a draught on the fire, and had a direct drive from the cylinders. In these fundamentals, the steam locomotive was to change little throughout its entire existence, despite the aspirations of innumerable individuals and design teams over subsequent years.

The advent of steam traction enabled industrial development, then in its infancy, to grow and spread with much greater speed than previously. At last, raw materials could be conveyed quickly and efficiently from source to manufacturer and from manufacturer to customer, while ordinary people found they were no longer confined to the small villages and market towns in which they were raised; in short, the social and industrial revolution thus wrought by the age of steam ensures it a fundamental place in world history.

This is not to propagandise for steam as much as for the transport system it created. The steam locomotive does have inherent weaknesses that, arguably, render it unsuitable for conditions in many countries, especially the developed ones. However, forsaking the railways altogether and basing national economies upon road transportation is untenable. The road system demands limitless financial resources in order to sustain it, while constituting a wanton dissipation of energy supplies. Future generations may well regard an overwhelming dependence upon road transport as one of the biggest acts of folly committed during the twentieth century.

During its development, the steam locomotive diversified into tens of thousands of different types. This incredible variety was due to two prime factors: firstly, railway systems large and small the world over invariably wanted their own designs, and secondly, throughout its entire evolution, locomotive designers were under constant pressure to enlarge and improve their products in the face of an unremitting demand for heavier and faster trains.

Another factor that ensured variety was the absence of any agreed international design, such as occurs with aeroplanes and road vehicles and other major forms of transport. Although heavy standardisation was achieved in a few countries, cross fertilisations were few and, when they did occur, were invariably due to war operations or reparation packages following a war. Of course, the private locomotive builders, particularly those specialising in industrial locomotives, had their own ranges of standard designs, but even these were varied to suit the needs (or fantasies) of the recipient. Also remarkable is the fact is that few condemned engines were ever sold to other countries. Although international differences in gauge sometimes inhibited such manoeuvres, there were still many instances where such sales might have taken place, but due to constantly changing operating conditions – the very thing that fostered diversity in the first place – such actions were usually rendered inappropriate.

The largest class of steam locomotive in world history was the Russian E 0-10-0, which totalled some 14,000 examples, and after these came the German Kriegslokomotive 2-10-0s, the Third Reich's workhorse of World War II; in basic form these totalled more than 6,000 examples. Teutonic precision had ensured earlier standardisations and the Prussian G8 0-8-0 and P8 4-6-0 numbered some 5,000 and 3,000 examples respectively. More recently, the Chinese have achieved comparable figures with their QJ class 2-10-2s, having over 4,000 units in service. These are all dramatic exceptions, however, as the vast majority of designs produced consisted of much smaller numbers, with an average of less than fifty examples per type.

Steam locomotives can be grouped into six basic categories according to the duties they were designed to perform. In order of evolution, the categories are as follows: industrial, freight, express passenger, shunting, suburban and cross country/mixed traffic.

Trains within the industrial category are quite distinct from any main-line operation, being confined to large industrial concerns, such as mines, docks, collieries, iron and steel works, quarries and power stations. Typically, these were small tank engines, but there were many fascinating exceptions to the rule, as the following pages reveal.

The main-line freight locomotive evolved in 1825 when *Locomotion* was used on the Stockton and Darlington Railway. Freight haulers were, by definition, tender engines which ranged from 0-6-0s to 0-8-0s in their formative years to huge 2-10-4s and even larger Mallets at the end of the steam age. Most were characterised by relatively small wheels, designed to provide maximum adhesion when starting with heavy loads.

Express passenger engines were even more highly specialised, and they had large wheels, which were necessary to keep the moving parts running at moderate speeds. The type began with the singles, gravitated to 2-4-0s and 4-4-0s by the end of the nineteenth century, reaching its ultimate in most parts of the world with the Pacific 4-6-2.

Shunting engines evolved with the marshalling yards and large sidings, which were established once railway networks had developed and an interchange of traffic movements became necessary. Like their industrial relations, they were invariably tank engines designed for maximum adhesion and easy manoeuvrability, although many down-graded and out-winded freight engines gravitated into shunting yards in later years.

After the main lines had been built, suburban and cross-country locomotives arrived to service the urban districts around the areas of concentrated manufacturing and commercial activity. Such suburban services were best worked by tank engines, as these were able to run easily in either direction and had small wheels in order to start rapidly after their frequent station stops. Cross-country engines served the secondary interconnecting lines that joined up the main arteries, as well as the branch lines built around the same time. These engines were often similar to those used on suburban work, although in later years many downgraded passenger types found a further lease of active life on these secondary lines.

Mixed traffic was primarily a manifestation of the twentieth century, when freight trains had increased in speed, and rationalisation within motive power fleets demanded engines suitable for a wide range of duties. Such engines ultimately fulfilled most requirements on many of the world's railways, with the exception of the fastest passenger trains and the heaviest of freight hauls.

Examples of all these categories remain active across the world as the revolutionary discovery of steam in nineteenth-century Britain was so far reaching and its consequences so traumatic that its vestiges could never be eradicated in a few years of modernisation. Soon, the steam locomotive will have been a prime mover in the world for more than two centuries, since many years have yet to elapse in some countries before the fires are dropped for the last time. Once everywhere that was anywhere had steam railways, and the veterans linger on in direct confrontation with today's microchip age.

It is to these survivors, the last true workhorses of the Industrial Revolution, that this book is devoted. Sadly, their numbers dwindle daily and always at the cost of diversity and antiquity, for although the steam locomotive's survival into the twenty-first century is assured, this will inevitably be in its more standardised forms. For sure, should it ever come back to the forefront of the world's transport systems, it will not be in the same beloved multiplicity of forms that grace these pages.

MOTIVE POWER DEPOTS

Motive power depots, or engine sheds in common parlance, were the powerhouses of Britain's Industrial Revolution. They were strategically located at important junctions, in large towns and throughout the industrial belts; here, within a space of little more than a few acres, would be concentrated the power for the region's prime transport needs. Motive power depots fulfilled two principal functions: firstly, they were responsible for rostering out locomotives for all the workings within their area, and secondly, they provided routine daily maintenance for the locomotives, as well as periodic servicing and basic repairs.

Each depot had its own allocation of locomotives, and these could range from several hundred at the larger sheds to less than a dozen at the smaller ones. Many large towns and important junctions had separate depots for passenger and freight operations, others in less important areas provided locomotives for a whole range of services. A fine example of motive-power zoning was at Crewe, where the North shed handled the top-link passenger power for the many routes radiating from that junction, whilst Crewe South depot handled the multiplicity of freight and shunting diagrams always associated with any important junction and marshalling yard. In the later years of steam, the tall, mechanical coaling plants were familiar landmarks and ready pointers to the whereabouts of these enchanting places.

Rostering was extremely complex and many locomotives would run for periods of several days, depots on the ongoing section of the various diagrams being responsible for fuelling and routine servicing as necessary.

Few people could fail to be thrilled by the atmosphere and intrigue of the engine sheds. The massive concentration of locomotives in close proximity there was positively awe-inspiring and the omnipresent tension of these gurgling giants unforgettable. These were places of intense and fervent activity, where locomotives coming in for coaling, watering, fireraking, oiling, sanding and turning contrasted with a steady stream of prepared steam locomotives going out to work. All of this happened alongside massive backup facilities that enabled others to receive boiler washouts and more extensive routine maintenance in the Sick Bay, as the repair area of the depot was known.

At the height of the steam age, the railway was the lifeblood of the economy and motive power depots were operative in varying degrees of intensity every day and night of the year. An average depot with an allocation of eighty locomotives would employ hundreds of men on a three-shift system around the clock, ranging from drivers and firemen to fitting staff, shed labourers of many grades, down to the junior cleaners who traditionally were beginning their long apprenticeship to becoming drivers. On the administrative side were the shed foreman and the many grades of chargehands, along with a clerical staff who handled everything from locomotive mileages to drivers' timecards. The whole operation would be under a shed master, who was answerable in turn to the divisional superintendents.

The depots themselves took many fascinating forms; some were round houses with the routes radiating from a common turntable in the centre, others were long houses in which the engines were placed one behind another on any number of tracks, whilst others were half round houses, again with the routes radiating from a common turntable. Whatever the form of depot, a section was always reserved for repairs and maintenance, with most of the really intense activity occurring in the shed yard.

The motive power depot was a creation of the steam age, required partly because of the magnitude of railway operations at that time, but also because of the labour intensiveness of the steam locomotive itself. A considerable number of depots were needed – as recently as 1950 there were over 350 in Britain alone. Today, the prime objective is to have the minimum number of depots, with locomotives constantly out on line, moving from stabling points and only visiting their home depot at infrequent intervals when periodic maintenance has to be carried out. Indeed, the whole emphasis of locomotive design now is to reduce such maintenance by modular construction of parts, the ultimate ideal being to keep locomotives permanently on line for the vast majority of their working lives.

Efficient though this may be, it has deprived the railway of one of its most fascinating aspects, for a concentration of many locomotives on shed comprised of both home engines and visitors, with their exotic aura of faraway places, has always been a source of joy and fascination for young and old alike.

A pair of Indonesian State Railways B51 Class 4-4-0s (facing page) boil up outside their depot at Rangkasbitung, in Northern Java. These oil-fired veterans are among the world's last outside cylinder 4-4-0s and clearly show their Prussian ancestry. The flags on the smoke box top of No. B5138 are part of the celebrations for Independence Day.

Above: two British thoroughbreds on shed at Olavarria, on the former Buenos Aires and Great Southern Railway network in Argentina. The one on the left is a IIA Class 2-8-0, alongside one of the splendid 15B Class 4-8-0s. The tragic decline of this once-magnificent railway is clearly in evidence, for the pride of the BAGS has been decimated by the petty profiteering of road hauliers with vested interests and by fifth column practices. The Scottish ancestry of this IIB Class 2-8-0 (right) is in full evidence, albeit that this example was one of the last batch delivered and came from the Vulcan Foundry at Newton-le-Willows, Lancashire, in 1931.

Left: a lively scene at the Sabero colliery in Northern Spain depicting a vintage Sharpe Stewart 0-6-0T *El Esla* of 1878 on the left, standing alongside an 0-6-0T built by Couillet of Belgium. This metre-gauge system is one of steam's last strongholds in Spain. Although steam building finished in India in 1972, major overhauls continue to this day. One of the principal works is in Jamalpur, where (bottom left) an HGS Class 2-8-0, descended from the BESA period, is seen alongside a WP Class Pacific. The two engines are preparing for running trials from Jamalpur shed, having received major overhauls. Two BESA-styled classics (below) at Lucknow receive the detailed embellishments so characteristic of Indian locomotives. The inside cylinder 0-6-0 on the left was built by Armstrong Whitworth of Newcastle-upon-Tyne in 1923, whilst the HPS Class 4-6-0 on the right came from the Vulcan Foundry in 1950. The once vast Howrah steam sheds in Calcutta had, until the late '70s, classic British designs both from the BESA and X series. Overleaf: an inside cylinder 0-6-0 *Maid of all Work* reposes alongside one of the magnificent XC Class Pacifics, introduced in 1928.

The Japanese sent many of their superbly styled designs to Taiwan when the island was under their occupation and known as Formosa. Perhaps the most interesting were these Japanese National Railway C57 Class Pacifics and this one (below) is depicted near the end of its working life at the Chia Yi depot on the west coast main line of the Taiwan Government Railway. Right: one of the Austrian State Railway's 77 Class 4-6-2Ts protrudes from the semi-round house at Linz. The unusual chimney indicates that she is fitted with a Giesl ejector, an Austrian innovation designed to improve draughting and reduce coal consumption. Overleaf: more Japanese standard designs on the Taiwan Government Railway's 3ft 6in gauge main lines featuring, from left to right, a 9600 Class 2-8-0, an 8620 Class 2-6-0 Mogul, and a latter day D51 Class 2-8-2 Mikado. The trio is seen boiling up for action at Hsinchu motive power depot on Taiwan's west coast main line.

One of China's finest steam centres is Harbin (above), in the north east of the country. Until the recent infiltration of diesels, the depot had an allocation of a hundred steam locomotives, of which most were QJs for working long distance freight trains, particularly to the south along the main line through Manchuria. Top right: locomotive utilisation is highly impressive; servicing activities are carried out with great rapidity and the engines returned to the main line with minimum delay. Right: the JS Class Mikado 2-8-2, one of the QJ's smaller sisters, reposes alongside an even smaller SY Class industrial Mikado. China's most modern Pacifics are the RM Class introduced in 1957, and No. 1228 (overleaf) is shown resting outside the half-round house at Changchun prior to working a semi-fast to Jilin.

One of Britain's last great industrial systems was based around Dalmellington in Ayrshire, where a stud of Andrew Barclay saddle tanks survived on various duties until the mid '70s. An ironworks was built in Dalmellington in 1845 and was served by collieries in the immediate area, which survived long after the foundries were closed down. The system connected with British Railways at Waterside, the site of the former ironworks – the most outlying colliery being at Pennyvenie, where West Ayr Area No. 21 (above), a standard 16in Andrew Barclay 0-4-0ST, can be seen sedately drawing a rake of freshly lifted coals. Notice that the first wagon is non-standard and is serving as an improvised tender for additional fuel capacity.

ENGINES OF BRITISH INDUSTRY

The industrial locomotive is quite distinct from its main-line counterpart and saw use in such places as collieries, quarries, foundries, docks, coking plants, power stations and large factories. These engines were seldom seen by the public at large, often being confined to industrial establishments off the beaten track or else lost within the maze of foundries and factories that were the central features of the major manufacturing belts of Britain. The world's first steam locomotive was an industrial. Built at an ironworks in South Wales in 1804, it was designed to convey iron to a canal basin for shipment by barge to the docks. A few years later, industrial engines began to appear on the coalfields of Yorkshire and Northumberland.

The origin of the industrial locomotive lay in the small engines built for the contractors who undertook the massive programme of construction throughout the 'railway mania' of the 1840s. These engines were needed to supplement the muscle power of the navvies and horses when building cuttings, embankments, tunnels, viaducts and stations. They had to be compact and economical, able to work over temporary track, negotiate tight curves and yet have sufficient adhesion to draw heavy trainloads of earth and materials. Additionally, the engines had to be easy to transport from one site to another. Small tank engines met all these requirements.

Once the main lines were laid, the Industrial Revolution progressed with increased velocity; enormous quantities of iron and coal were required and these very industries needed the same type of locomotives as the contractors did. Thus, by 1850, the industrial steam locomotive, as it appears in these pages, had evolved.

The basic form was a side or a saddle tank, which had either four or six coupled wheels (0-4-0 and 0-6-0) with two cylinders, usually placed inside the frame. Outside cylinder versions did occur, particularly on the four-wheelers, where the short boiler provided insufficient room for a crank axle. These engines changed little throughout their evolution, growing within moderate limits both in terms of power output and size, and seldom exceeding fifty tonnes in weight.

Industrial engines are associated with the towns in which their builders were located. In Scotland, the coal and ironstone reserves of Ayrshire gave work to builders in Kilmarnock, pre-eminent amongst whom was Andrew Barclay, who produced highly distinctive locomotives for almost a century.

In Newcastle-upon-Tyne Robert Stephenson and Hawthorn Leslie both produced highly distinctive designs, but the true home of the industrial locomotive was Leeds, where in the tiny parish of Hunslet there were four celebrated builders: Manning Wardle, Hudswell Clarke, Kitsons and Hunslet. Further south, in Stafford, William Bagnall readily tailored his designs to customer requirements and as a result this company's list contains some of the most delightful variations ever played on the conventional theme. Meanwhile, in the deep south, a distinctive family of engines arose from the designs of Peckett and Avonside in Bristol.

Sadly, the combination of closures, rationalisations in plant layouts and the increasing use of trucks and overhead cranes within all aspects of heavy industry has lead to a drastic decline in the number of locations using industrials, as has the the main-line railway's use of merry-go-round trains to service industries such as power stations and collieries direct. So although steam survived in industry for some years after it had disappeared from mainline service, diesels rapidly encroached on the surviving locations and today, after almost two centuries of operation, the industrial locomotive is extinct in Britain. These engines preceded their main-line counterparts by some twenty years and survived them by approximately the same timespan.

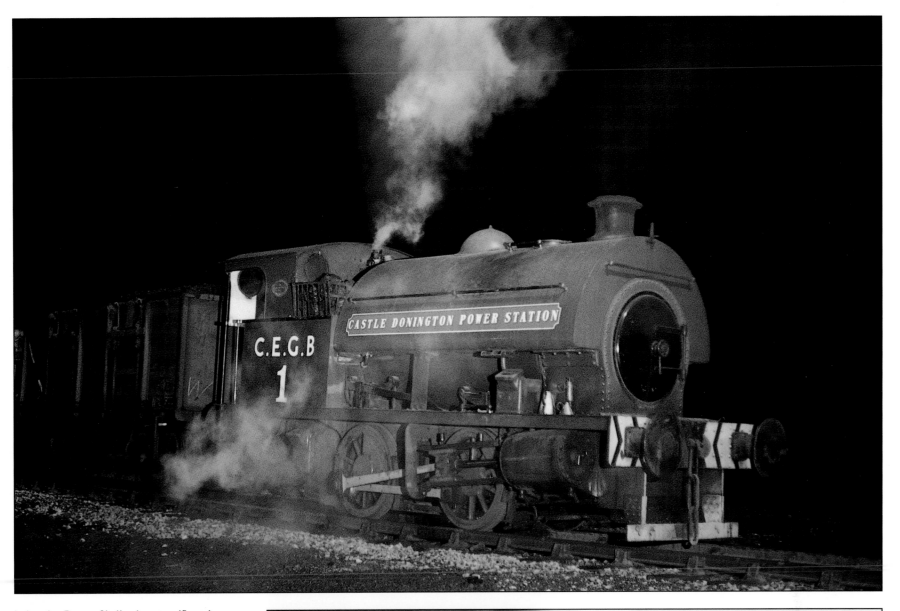

Leicester Power Station's magnificent
Robert Stephenson and Hawthorn 0-4-0
saddle tank (facing page) gently backs a
rake of loaded wagons from the British Rail
Exchange into the power station hoppers.
She was built as recently as 1950 to a
Hawthorn Leslie design dating from the
early years of the century. She has twelve-
inch-diameter cylinders, and slide valves
operated by Stephenson's link motion.
Castle Donington Power Station, also in
Leicestershire, is home to a pair of blue-
liveried RSH 0-4-0STs, also descended from
an earlier Hawthorn Leslie design. The
family likeness between the Hawthorn 0-4-0
saddle tank and the RSH 0-4-0ST (above) is
unmistakable, although the latter has
sixteen-inch-diameter cylinders. This
powerful 0-6-0T (right), seen towards the
end of her working life in the Glenboig
colliery in Glasgow, comes from the Leeds
school of industrial locomotive development, having originally come from
Hudswell Clarke in 1909.

The one-and-three-quarter-century-long tradition of steam and coal – the lifeblood of the industrial revolution – ended in Britain during the early 1980s at the Cadley Hill colliery on the Derbyshire coalfield. Among Cadley Hill's fleet was *Empress* (above), a standard 16in Bagnall design which first appeared in 1944, although descended from an earlier similar design. Two other members (left) of Cadley Hill's fleet can still be seen, a Hunslet Austerity on the left, *Cadley Hill No 1*, alongside *Progress*, a Robert Stephenson and Hawthorn 0-6-0 saddle tank, built in Newcastle in 1946. As with the 0-4-0s on previous pages, she is also descended from an earlier Hawthorn Leslie design and is unusual in having inside cylinders. *Cadley Hill No 1* (facing page) was one of the last three Hunslet Austerities to be built and didn't emerge from Hunslet's Leeds works until 1962. The Hunslet Austerity was specially designed for operations during World War II, after which many passed to the metals of the newly formed National Coal Board, to become a standard design and ultimately the last working steam locomotives in Britain.

Beneath a magnificent layer of grime, a vintage Andrew Barclay 0-6-0 saddle tank of 1900 (above) pauses at the British Railways exchange for a blow up, having drawn a rake of loaded wagons from the Polkemment colliery in West Lothian. The crane tank was a form of industrial which combined an ability to shunt works yards with an ability to load wagons and move heavy items around the various fabrication shops. Among Britain's last working examples is the 0-4-0 CT (right) which survived, with a few others, at Doxford's shipyard in Pallion, Sunderland, until 1971.

One of the many instances of former mainline engines being transferred to industrial service occurs in the case of the ex-Great Western 5700 Class 0-6-0 pannier tank (above), sold by British Railways to the National Coal Board and seen here ending her days at the Mountain Ash colliery in South Wales. Facing page: a Hunslet Austerity with a Giesl chimney at work on the Fifeshire coalfield.

ENGINES OF WORLD INDUSTRY

In world terms, the industrial locomotive differed considerably from those confined to Britain. Generally they were more powerful, as wagon sizes were often heavier than those in Britain and the industries themselves invariably larger. Britain's small size, combined with her diversity of industries, which developed piecemeal under private enterprise during the formative years of the Industrial Revolution, had much to do with this. Small industrial units serving a densely populated area of heavy manufacturing were sustainable, but in less developed countries, industries tended to be larger, more spread out and located at longer distances from the mainline railway. This, combined with poor and often heavily graded track, necessitated a very different kind of locomotive from the homely British saddletank that worked at the local gasworks.

Many world industrials were, of course, similar to their British counterparts in terms of power output, and Britain did export such locomotives to many lands. On a world canvas, these readily mixed with a massive quantity of German engines from such pre-eminent builders as Orenstein and Koppel, with their huge family of characteristically shaped designs, as well as with those locomotives from American plants as large as Baldwins, to the smaller foundries that specialised in industrials, like Lima of Ohio. Although industrial locomotives were used across the world in similar establishments to the ones in Britain, there are two additional major locations – sugar plantations and logging lines – which even today rely on steam locomotives to convey their raw materials from the cutting areas to the factories. These systems are invariably built to narrow gauges ranging from 2ft 6in to 3ft 6in.

Some of the world's largest industrials occur in South Africa, where the main-line gauge is only 3ft 6in, but here it is free of the loading gauge restrictions that apply in more developed areas of the world. This enables locomotives and rolling stock to be built higher and wider, as often the coalfield hauls are heavier than were the average main-line hauls in Europe at the end of steam – and this over track beds that are often much more steeply graded. Many of these locomotives are former mainliners and, as such, reveal another fascinating category of industrials: the engines that have seen service, either on the privately owned or state main-line systems, and are pensioned off into industry for a further lease of active life. This cross-fertilisation of different types of locomotives was aided by the steady increase in tonnages – thus an engine built in the late-nineteenth century to handle the heaviest main-line freight hauls of the day was inadequate fifty years later. These engines are either demoted to lighter work, such as tripping and shunting, or else offered for sale to industrial users as an alternative to being broken up.

Through this method, many historic types which would otherwise have become extinct long since have lingered in industrial establishments, sometimes for incredibly long periods of time. As the stresses and demands upon an industrial can be relatively modest, given good maintenance many seem to go on forever. Large mainline engines seldom penetrated the ranks of British industry, but they certainly made inroads elsewhere; in Africa, Latin America, on the Indian subcontinent and in China many large locomotives, some of them extremely powerful, have found a new lease of life. These contrast magnificently with the traditional, smaller designs, providing a tapestry of interesting locomotives across a rich diversity of locations.

The stone railway at Gunung Kataren, Sumatra, is one of the world's most remarkable industrial lines. Its purpose is to convey stones from the river bed up to the crushing plant in order to provide track ballast for the island's mainline railways. The smooth stones are clearly visible as engine No. 106 (above), an 0-6-0T built in 1926 by Ducroo and Brauns of Weesp, Holland, prepares to back a loaded train to the crushers.

The yellow-flowering trees of Java make a fine backdrop for *Bromo* (above), an Orenstein and Kopell 0-8-0 tender tank of 1913, as it works for the Purwodadi sugar factory in the eastern part of the island, its tender piled high with cubes of bagasse . Another German-built industrial, a diminutive 600mm gauge 0-4-0 well tank (top right), also from Orenstein and Kopell, heads a loaded train from a stone quarry in central Uruguay. The barrel precariously perched atop the boiler indicates that she is an oil burner. Right: the world's last Kitson Meyer 0-6-6-0T at Taltal, in Chile's Atacama Desert. Notice the rear chimney protruding from the bunker and exhausting steam from the rear cylinders. Overleaf: *Don Carlos*, a 2-8-2 well tank built in 1916 by Manning Wardle of Leeds, resting on a 2ft 6in gauge industrial railway in the wilds of the Paraguayan Chaco.

One of South Africa's most fascinating and antiquated industrials was Albion colliery's No. 3 (above), a hybridised 4-8-0 tender engine rebuilt from a 13 Class 4-10-2T supplied by Neilson of Glasgow in 1902. Top right: a very different No. 3 at the East Daggafontein goldmine. Originally a mainliner, she was a member of the Natal Government Railway A Class, which consisted of a hundred engines built by the Dubs works in Queens Park, Glasgow, between 1888 and 1900. Right: another former Natal Government Railway Class A, active on the Grootvlei Proprietary Mines goldfield at Springs, in the Transvaal. The handsome 4-8-2 (overleaf) is a marvellous example of a mainline design being adapted for industrial service. Introduced in 1919 as a heavy freight design, building continued in unsuperheated form for colliery service until well into the 1950s.

Vast reserves of iron ore underlie India's Bihar Province, and these feed the great iron and steel works on the eastern coalfield of Bengal. At Manoharpur, two Andrew Barclay 0-6-2Ts (below) head along the branch from the mines to the South Eastern Railway's main line. Right: the Indian Iron and Steel Corporation's Burnpur works in Bengal, where No. 9, a 2-6-0T built by Nasmyth Wilson of Patricroft, Manchester, waits for the cauldron to be filled. Bottom right: No. 17, a heavy-duty 0-6-0 tank built by Robert Stephenson and Hawthorn in 1948, also in the Burnpur works. Overleaf: a 1937 heavy-duty Bagnall 0-8-0T standing by at the Karabuk steelworks in northern Turkey.

These pages: slag tipping at Karabuk steelworks, northern Turkey. A stream of molten waste (top left) pours down a bank as one of Karabuk's stud of British-built 0-6-0 saddle tanks eases the wagons into place. She was built in 1948 by Robert Stephenson and Hawthorn, but is descended from an earlier Hawthorn Leslie design delivered for the steelworks' opening in 1937. Left: one of the huge Bagnall 0-8-0s performs a spectacular night tip. Above: a Robert Stephenson and Hawthorn 0-6-0ST of 1948. Although the huge moulded forms of solidified slag have cooled on the outside, in many cases their centres are still liquid. Overleaf: the striking contrasts of slag-tipping at twilight, with the typical shape of a Hawthorn Leslie engine, virtually identical to that builder's designs for British industrial establishments, silhouetted against the early evening sky.

Above: one of the Indonesian State Railway B53 Class 4-4-0s. These were superheated versions of the earlier B51 Class and were built for the 3ft 6in gauge Staats Spoorwegen. The class numbered eleven examples, delivered from Hartmann of Germany in 1912 and Werkspoor of Holland in 1914. Once the express locomotives of the Dutch East Indies, the last B53s ended their days working indiscriminately with the older B50 Class Sharp Stewart 2-4-0s on the lightly laid branch from Madiun to Ponorogo and Slahung.

COALING, WATERING AND MAINTAINING

Many indictments have been made against steam traction during the second half of the twentieth century, but perhaps the most damning is the labour-intensive maintenance it demands. Unlike the internal combustion engine, it does not start at the touch of a button, but only after the fire has been lit, and it is many hours before steam is finally raised. Alongside this are the attendant activities of fireraking, coaling, watering and regular oiling for every trip. Equally, the steam locomotive does not switch off when its duty roster is completed; a decision has to be made whether to drop the fire or keep the engine in light steam until it is needed again. Light steam maintenance demands that the engine be visited regularly in order to keep the fire banked up and the boiler topped with water, but so time-consuming is the process of raising steam that this constant use of energy and manpower is the preferred alternative to dropping the fire if a locomotive is needed within the following twelve hours or so.

The situation was made even more complex at the end of every run, as then a locomotive would have to be replenished with coal – sometimes as much as ten tonnes. It had to be watered, have its fire raked and ashpan cleaned, and the deposits of char shovelled from the smoke box. Also, in the majority of cases, the locomotive would have to be turned, and all these operations necessitated going to a depot. The availability of water throughout the railway network was not usually a problem in developed countries, but it could be in many parts of the developing world, and, of course, the movement of vast tonnages of coal from the areas of production to every motive power depot across the country was in itself a massive and costly operation. Some of these difficulties were minimised by the introduction of water troughs between the tracks, from which the engines scooped up water at speed, whilst mechanical coaling plants, rocking grates and self-cleaning smokeboxes were all attributes of latter-day steam practice, as was the introduction of oil-firing. Nevertheless, such labour intensiveness was inherent, for once an engine had left a depot, having been sent on its way by a multifarious workforce, it demanded the constant attention of a driver and fireman.

Air pollution – an emotive issue in the developed world following World War II – was another factor in the decline of steam traction there. The steam locomotive was seen as part of the blackened (and thus unacceptable) legacy from the days of the 'Dark Satanic Mills'. After the war, serious competition from road transportation reared its ugly head, forcing railway networks to modernise and present a new image of competitiveness. This could hardly be achieved as long as trains were hauled by soot-laden, clanking monsters that belched smoke and fumes into the atmosphere. In Western countries, the dirty work associated with running a steam railway also became unfashionable; it was considered unreasonable for a man to be obliged to stand for hours shovelling tonnes of coal in clammy heat on a bucking locomotive or, equally, to suffer the dust and fumes involved in fireraking. Steam locomotive depots, characterised by their pall of smoke mushrooming skywards, became blots on the landscape in a world suddenly conscious of pollution. Additionally, the postwar years were a time of cheap oil, but ever more expensive coal; in many countries a ready availability of high quality steam coal was becoming increasingly difficult to guarantee.

If all these factors are considered against the availability of diesel and electric traction, the utilisation figures for steam compare unfavourably; after all, one diesel can do the work of almost three steam locomotives.

However, steam traction has many pluses: it is cheap to build, simple to maintain and incredibly reliable. It will continue to work well under conditions of adversity that no other form of traction would tolerate – and however bad its ailments, a steam locomotive will almost invariably drag the train home. This contrasts markedly with diesel or electrical traction, where a small technical failure can paralyse a locomotive, or even a whole system. These factors are important in developing countries, where the maintenance of modern forms of traction frequently causes serious problems, but perhaps the fundamental factor in steam traction's favour is the spirit which the steam locomotive generates in man. It is an animated, living machine comprising the fundamental elements of fire and water. Each locomotive has an individual personality to which man can readily respond, and as such it presents a challenge to him, and almost always brings out the best in him. One example of this is the way that a late-running train can be returned to schedule by the driver and firemen coaxing the locomotive to a stupendous performance, much as a skilled jockey coaxes a racehorse. All this introduces an esprit de corps which must be at the heart of any great industry; this and the steam locomotive's capacity to inspire workforce, travelling public and layman alike are facts which are readily forgotten by economists and accountants. The spirit, the dedication and the loyalties once inspired by steam are absent on the modern railways of today and the industry is very much the poorer as a consequence.

Left: a Yugoslav State Railway B51 Class 2-6-2T takes water at Vrginmost as it travels along the lightly laid branch from Sisak to Karlovac. Above: a former Rhodesian Railways 2-6-2+2-6-2 Garratt takes water at Balla Balla, on the West Nicholson to Bulawayo line. As the giant takes refreshment, the blow-down valve is simultaneously opened to eject sludge from the boiler. Eighteen of these 132-tonne giants were exported from Beyer Peacock's works in Gorton, Manchester, between 1953 and 1954. Overleaf: No. 6024, a former East African Railways 60 Class 4-8-2+2-8-4 Garratt, pauses for refreshment on its journey towards Voi with an overnight mixed freight from Moshi in Tanzania. Known colloquially as 'The Governors', the 60s were named after the British governors who at one time controlled Kenya, Uganda, and Tanganyika. This locomotive once bore the name *Sir James Hayes-Sadler* but this, along with all other such splendid-sounding names, was removed after the nations' independence.

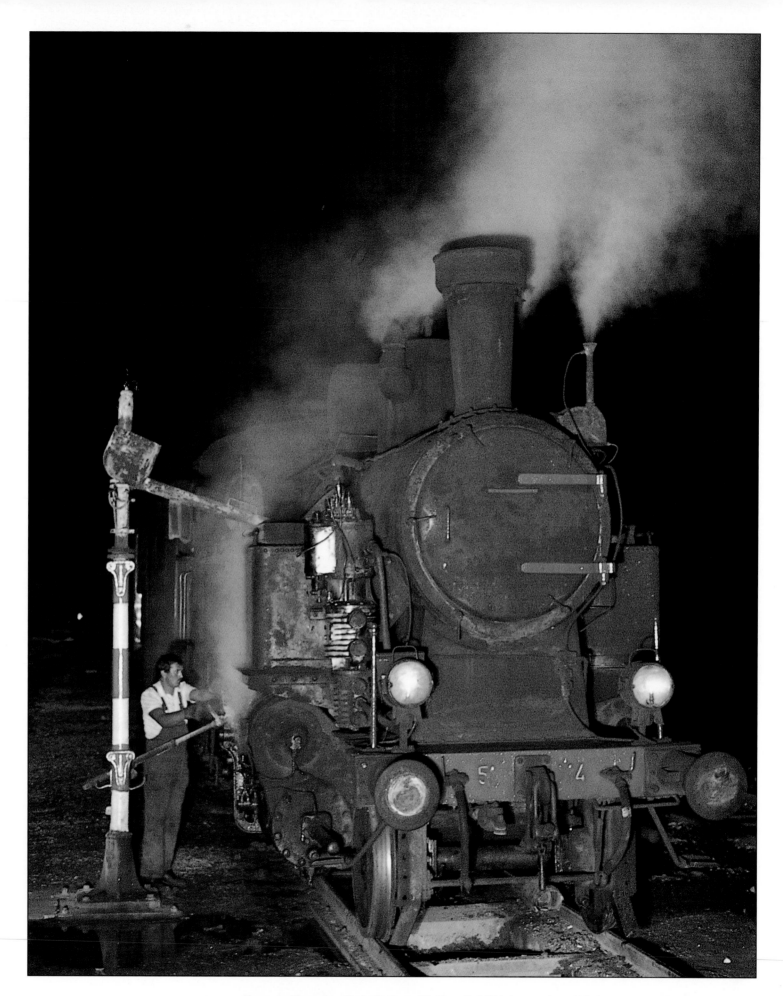

Above: a Yugoslav State Railway 51 Class 2-6-2T takes water at Vrginmost on its journey drawing the overnight passenger train from Karlovac to Sisak. Yugoslavia ran many former Austrian-designed engines, one of the most common being the 25 Class 2-8-0 (facing page). Some 500 were built, and the type saw service in many East European countries following the dismemberment of the Austro-Hungarian Empire.

The modern, thriving town of Karlovac, in Croatia, seems an unlikely location in which to find veteran locomotives dating back to the days of the Austro-Hungarian Empire, but several Yugoslav State Railway 51 Class 2-6-2Ts (above) are retained for working the lightly laid branch to Sisak. The section between Karlovac and Vrginmost was opened in 1907, and it is possible that these locomotives, with their eleven-tonne axle loadings, have worked the line since its inception. The heavy maintenance work on No. 51.028 (right) at Karlovac requires char deposits to be shovelled from her smoke box. She was built for the Croatian State Railways in 1926.

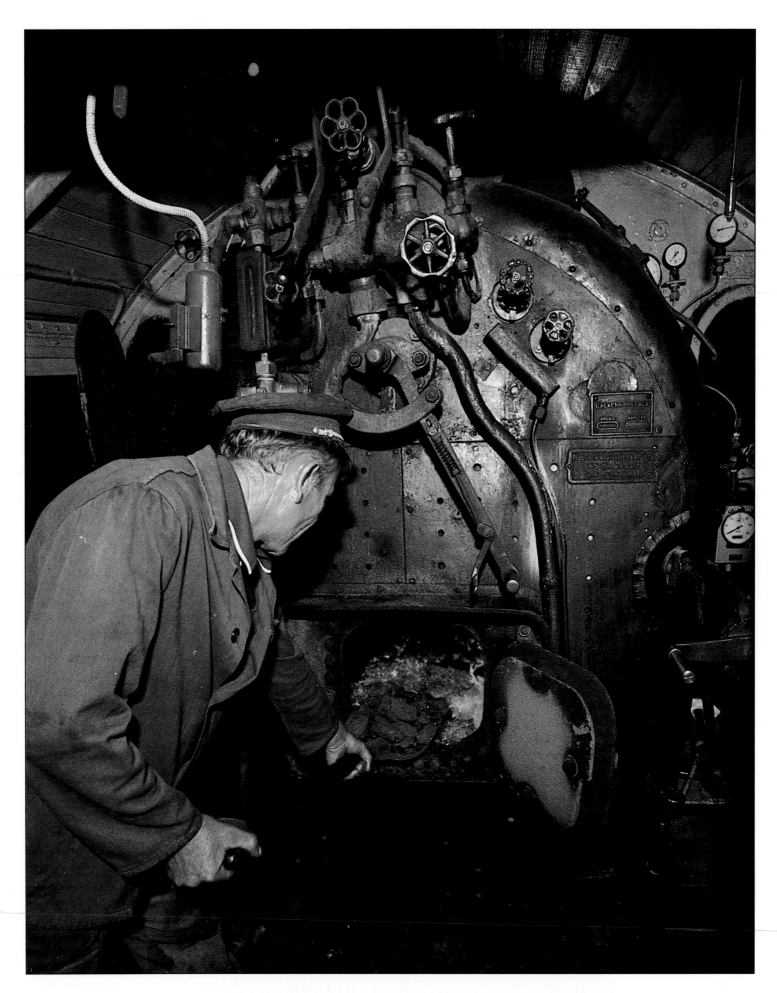

A shedman adds a round of coal to the firebox of Yugoslav State Railway's Class 20 No. 131 (above) as his mate shovels hot ashes from her smokebox (facing page). This engine is one of several Class 20 locomotives which survive on the lightly laid cross-country line from Sid in Serbia to Bijeljina in Bosnia.

The world's last main line worked entirely by steam engines spans the 232 miles from the Paraguayan capital Asuncion to Encarnacion on the Argentinian border. The line is known grandly as the 'Ferrocarril Presidente Carlos Antonio Lopez', and exhibits a variety of engines, among which are fine period 2-6-2 tanks built by Hawthorn Leslie in Newcastle-upon-Tyne between 1910 and 1913. The class numbered six engines which were built in unsuperheated form with slide valves. Above: No. 5 at Encarnacion, waiting to push wagons onto the decks of a paddle steamer for conveyance over the River Parana to the connection with Argentina's standard gauge Urquiza Railway.

ON THE MAIN LINES

Few people under the age of forty appreciate the flamboyance of the great age of steam. The steam locomotive is generally regarded as belonging to the distant past, related to the Victorian era rather than the modern world. In the popular mind of today, the steam train was slow and dirty, albeit charming, and in the interests of true progress it was an inevitable casualty. Nothing could be further from the truth. As recently as forty years ago, before the age of the motorway and the juggernaut, railways were the principal form of transport and a large percentage of the world's main lines were worked by steam. In postwar Britain, before the road economy became established, some 20,000 steam locomotives formed a safe, properly co-ordinated and disciplined form of transport which moved the nation's freight with speed and efficiency and provided passenger journeys to virtually every corner of the island.

This flamboyance has been lost as the steam age has declined across the world. The survivors are now sedate plodders and, but for very rare exceptions, are only found on humble duties, generally eking out their time until more recent forms of motive power can be introduced. This belies the inherent ability of steam traction, for as long ago as the 1840s, speeds faster than a mile a minute were well authenticated on Brunel's seven foot gauges. Before the end of the century, the railway races from London to Scotland produced some incredible performances: trains reached Aberdeen from London in as little as eight-and-a-half hours. This scintillating part of railway history also produced the run by the LNWR Jumbo 2-4-0 number 792 *Hardwick*, which achieved an average speed of just over sixty-seven miles per hour over the 144 miles from Crewe to Carlisle.

Three figure speeds were reached soon after the turn of the century, when the Great Western Railway's 4-4-0 *City of Truro* made its epic run down Wellington Bank and reached 102.3 miles an hour, but the 1930s must surely be regarded as the finest decade for world steam performance, as these years saw the *Cheltenham Flyer* cover the seventy-seven miles from London Paddington to Swindon in fifty-six minutes – a feat that earned it the title 'The World's Fastest Train'. Even more impressive were the attainments of the streamlined locomotives of the Thirties; in America high-speed Atlantics on the Chicago Milwaukee St. Paul and Pacific Railroad worked the *Hiawatha Express* over its 431-mile run from Chicago to Milwaukee in 400 minutes, including intermediate stops. To achieve this, sustained speeds in excess of a hundred miles an hour were normal. It was during the streamlined era in Britain that the world's speed record for steam traction was attained by Nigel Gresley's LNER Pacific *Mallard*, which reached a speed of 126 miles an hour on the descent of Stoke Bank between Grantham and Peterborough.

The popular characterisation of a steam locomotive crawling along with a heavy goods train is also far from representative of the age. Heavy mineral trains were characteristically slow, but from the early years of this century, mixed commodity trains worked at speeds that would compare favourably with those achieved on the motorway trucking routes of today. It is hard to conceive a time when virtually every commodity was moved by rail, being coordinated on its journey through marshalling yards, which achieved a breathtaking rate of efficiency, or else travelling directly via such epic freight trains as the overnight Grimsby fish hauls, which had fish that had been landed at Grimsby in the afternoon on the fishmonger's slab in London the following morning. In those days, the famous four o'clock Scotch goods from King's Cross ran on passenger train timings and carried hundreds of tonnes of freight with a rapidity and ease unheard of in today's road-orientated society.

In these pages, the last epic fling of the steam locomotive age is remembered. In Britain, this occurred on the Southern Region of British Railways, as services from London (Waterloo) to Southampton, Bournemouth and Weymouth were exclusively handled by steam as recently as 1967. The stars of these dramas were Bulleid's rebuilt Pacifics, and during the final year regular speeds of a hundred miles an hour were attained by engine crews conscious that a tradition was coming to its close. In Europe, steam flamboyance lasted longer and went out in a blaze of glory in the German Democratic Republic in 1977, when the magnificent 01 Class Pacifics of 1925 ceased working the express runs between Berlin and Dresden. Until that year, the 103-mile journey was regularly covered at scheduled speeds in excess of sixty miles an hour with loads of up to 400 tonnes, reaching top speeds of ninety miles an hour.

Today, hardly anything survives of steam's gallant performances. Exceptions occur in India, where the stalwart WP Pacifics are diagrammed to work expresses which sometimes reach speeds of seventy miles an hour and have short bursts of mile-a-minute timings, and to a lesser degree in China, where the magnificent RM and SL Class Pacifics occasionally reach a mile a minute with their increasingly heavy trains. The steam locomotive was the workhorse of the Industrial Revolution and possessed all the stolid characteristics of the reliable carthorse, but it was also a greyhound. Its ability to produce such differing performances with consummate ease is yet another aspect of its allure.

The Prussian P8 Class 4-6-0 was one of the most celebrated models in locomotive history and played an important part in the Prussian State Railway's standardisation scheme. The first example appeared in 1906, and by the 1930s almost 4,000 were in operation. They were the first superheated 4-6-0s to appear and, in many respects, they set the trend for the introduction of other 4-6-0s throughout Europe. They survived into the 1970s. Left: a Prussian P8 at Horb, in the Black Forest. The German Class 44 three-cylinder 2-10-0 (above) was almost as celebrated as the P8; some 2,000 were built, and they saw service in many countries during and after World War II. A supremely successful design, the 44s were capable of hauling 2,000-tonne trains along level track at thirty-five miles an hour. One of their last haunts was the Mosel Valley route from Koblenz to Trier. Overleaf: a German Class 44 shown crossing the Mosel against a backdrop of the region's celebrated vineyards.

Britain's last steam-hauled expresses survived on the London Waterloo to Southampton, Bournemouth and Weymouth line until 1967. Top left: a rebuilt Merchant Navy Class Pacific No. 35007, *Aberdeen Commonwealth*, passes Worthing junction, and (left) an ex Great Western Class 1600 0-6-0 pannier tank at Tyseley. Above: a former Great Western Class 4500 branch-line prairie tank, No. 4555, resting in the preserved Dart Valley Railway in Devon. Overleaf: an ex LNER A4 Class Pacific No. 4498, *Sir Nigel Gresley*, returns to Bournemouth Central in readiness for working an enthusiasts' special to London Waterloo.

Facing page: the daily mixed from Sisak to Karlovac storms away from Vrginmost behind a Yugoslav State Railway 51 Class 2-6-2T, originally built in 1915 for the Hungarian State Railways. Yugoslavia's 20 Class 2-6-0 Moguls were designed by Borsig of Berlin, who were noted for building locomotives of a distinctly British appearance. The 20s were originally created to further Germany's imperialist aims to dominate, with the aid of her Turkish allies, all the territories from Berlin to Baghdad. They were carefully designed to be capable of working in all conditions over the difficult routes through Turkey and onwards to Baghdad. Above: a Yugoslav 20 Class 2-6-0 Mogul, and (right) a Yugoslav State Railway 28 Class 0-10-0, one of the country's famous designs inherited from the Austrian Empire.

The lines radiating from Izmir, on Turkey's Aegean coast, have long been celebrated for their fascinating variety of locomotive types; for example, a former Ottoman Railway 2-8-2 (above), built at Robert Stephenson's works in Newcastle-upon-Tyne, draws a mixed train along the line to Denizli. Right: a suburban train toils the heavy grades away from Izmir behind a 2-8-0, built in 1912 by Humboldt of Paris. Among Turkey's surviving steam fleet are some German Kriegslokomotives which date from World War II. The light axle loading of these trains allows them to work a wide variety of routes. They are regarded as mixed-traffic engines, working both passenger and freight duties, as well as mixed trains. The Kriegslokomotive engine shown leaving Egridir (overleaf) was built by the Maschinenbau und Bahnbedarf AG of Berlin at the height of the war in 1943.

These pictures of Poland's fabulous high-stepping PT47 Class Mikado 2-8-2s (these pages and overleaf) were taken at a line-side base near Kamieniec in the summer of 1983. These engines were responsible for some of the last express passenger duties in Europe; they have large-diameter driving wheels and the sleek characteristics of a Pacific, but as Mikados they pull away more quickly from station stops and climb gradients with more ease. The class numbered 180 examples, built between the late 1940s and early 1950s by the Polish builders Cegielski and Chrzanòw, and are descended from a 1920s design. The PT47s are important historically in being the finest surviving examples of the Polish school of locomotive design, which flowered after the First World War when Poland emerged as a united and self-governing country.

In a world in which the steam engine is relegated to relatively menial duties, the striking sights on China Railways' main lines, where an army of 4,500 QJ Class engines perform their arduous duties, are hard to believe. Above: a QJ Class 2-10-2 storms Wang Gang Bank south of Harbin with a train loaded with wood from the forests of the northeast, and (top right) a QJ heads southwards from Anshan along the main line to Dalian, with Saddle Mountain in the background. On the same journey, another QJ (right) heads for the port at Dalian in winter, towing an oil train. The contrast between exhaust effects, caused by the differences in winter and summer air, are marked. Overleaf: a QJ running wrong line, slides down the bank into Anshan with a heavy freight from the Port of Dalian, on the Yellow Sea coast.

The beauty of Portugal's Douro Valley makes a perfect setting for an inside cylinder 4-6-0 (above) easing a freight train into Ferradosa, en-route to Barca d'Alva on the Spanish frontier. These 5ft 6in gauge period pieces are among the most handsome locomotives in Europe and were part of a class of six engines delivered in 1910 from Henschel of Germany for the Portuguese State Railways.

The status of steam traction around the world is directly related to national affluence. Predictably, the first countries to eradicate steam were the USA and Canada, followed closely by Scandinavia and Western Europe, where steam traction is rapidly heading for extinction. The Western economies are all closely related in terms of social, technical and economic development, so in the related economies of Japan, Australia and New Zealand, the steam age has also passed into history. A very different situation applies in the developing world. Here societies are necessarily more disparate, not technically inter-related and, with the massive social problems in these lands, 'make do and mend' is the over-riding philosophy.

In France, steam has all but vanished and yet, within the last twenty years, four-cylinder Pacifics were working up to Calais with international trains and the 141R Class Mikados, supplied by American builders as aid to France's devastated railways following the ravages of World War II, could be found in many parts of the country. Even a few work-weary 140C Class 2-8-0s dating back to World War I remained active around the old battlefield regions of Verdun.

West German mainline steam survived into the 1970s with 2-10-0s, 2-8-2s and Pacifics – all German standard designs of the 1920s – active in various parts of the country, but especially on the busy line from Rheine to Emden. Another famous route was the scenic line through the Mosel Valley from Koblenz to Trier, which reverberated with the roar of three-cylinder 2-10-0s of 1920s vintage hauling trains in excess of 1,500 tonnes.

Steam lasted even longer on the Iberian Peninsula, and with a far greater diversity of types and gauges. During the early 1960s Spain had one of the most varied and antiquated locomotive fleets on earth; although the main lines were standardised at 5ft 6in, at least five other gauges could be found in use on secondary railways throughout the country. The boom in foreign tourism that began in the late Fifties transformed Spain's economy, and a lot of the money earned was used to modernise the railways, resulting in many of the antiquities vanishing within a few short years. The dawn of the Seventies, though, still found the country running massive 4-8-0s, 4-8-2s and 2-8-2s and a sprinkling of older types on shunting and trip work. The extensive coal-mining areas of the northwest remained havens for innumerable veterans; a handful survive today, though others lie derelict.

Neighbouring Portugal's main lines were also built to a 5ft 6in gauge, and services on the scenic Douro Valley route, which ran from Oporto on the Atlantic coast to Barca d'Alva on the Spanish frontier, was a haven for the world's last inside cylinder 4-6-0s. Portugal also had a large network of metre gauge secondary lines, some of which fed into the Douro Valley and sported 2-4-6-0 Mallets with copper-capped chimneys and gleaming brasswork.

Even more exciting were the metre gauge suburban services around Oporto, as here was a varied fleet of copper-capped antiquities in service on an intensively used network. With smoke-filled tunnels, vintage coaching stock and shrieking, panting locomotives, these services represented the last fling of the classic Victorian suburban railway.

Italy also ran a fine fleet of vintage locomotives, all based around a series of standard designs which evolved as long ago as 1905, when the country's railways were nationalised. Ostensibly, these were all out of use by the early 1980s, but, as isolated steam workings can still be found, the true situation remains an enigma.

In Scandinavia, Norway and Sweden were only a few years behind the USA in declaring against steam traction, although in Finland it survived much longer and the early Seventies saw a fine fleet of locomotives comprised of 2-8-0s, 2-8-2s and Pacifics. Even when these were replaced, many were mothballed in strategic reserves around the country. During the intervening years, some of these have been broken up and others purchased for preservation, but large numbers still remain on abandoned lines in forested areas.

The traveller in search of working steam in Western Europe today will find little to satisfy him, although industrial lines still yield some delightful discoveries. Odd survivors exist in West Germany, where Fireless locomotives can also be found in a variety of industrial locations. The Fireless also lingers on in Austria, but the high spot of Western Europe must be Switzerland, where the SLM works recently contracted to build three new steam locomotives for one of the country's narrow gauge lines.

In the Warsaw Pact countries of centralised economies, labour and fuel costs are equated on a different scale and railways remain pre-eminent over road transportation. In these countries, a general abundance of coal and a lack of oil ensured that steam not only survived, but remained free from commercial pressures for change. The result was that steam traction survived much longer behind the Iron Curtain and 0149 Class 2-6-2s can still be found in active mainline service in Poland, as can German Kriegslokomotive 2-10-0s and the fabulous passenger hauling PT47 Class 2-8-2 Mikados. In the German Democratic Republic, Krieglokomotives still appear on the odd secondary line, although this country is now more revered for its narrow gauge systems, which, though slowly declining, still sport a fascinating variety of designs on delightfully rural systems.

Hewn from the territorial carve-up of the Austro-Hungarian Empire following World War I, Yugoslavia is a land of great territorial complexity. Its locomotive history reflects this; the country was, until recent years, host to one of the most varied and fascinating motive power fleets on earth. Here, classics of Austrian, Hungarian, and Serbian design mixed with the standard types ultimately created for Yugoslavia proper, while added to these was a wide variety of war designs, many of which came in the form of reparations from both the world wars. Although much of the complexity has been swept away in recent years, it is still possible to see Serbian Moguls working turn and turn about with Hungarian 2-6-2 tanks of early twentieth-century origin, and contrasting with such classic wartime designs as the United States Army Transportation Corps 0-6-0Ts of World War II. Yugoslavian industrial lines are havens for a few rare and obsolete types, but these – in common with the railways of the Warsaw Pact countries – are generally hazardous to visit, or else inaccessible.

Above: *El Elsa*, the veteran Sharp Stewart 0-6-0T at Sabero colliery in northern Spain, emerges from a tunnel with a coal train bound for the RENFE exchange.

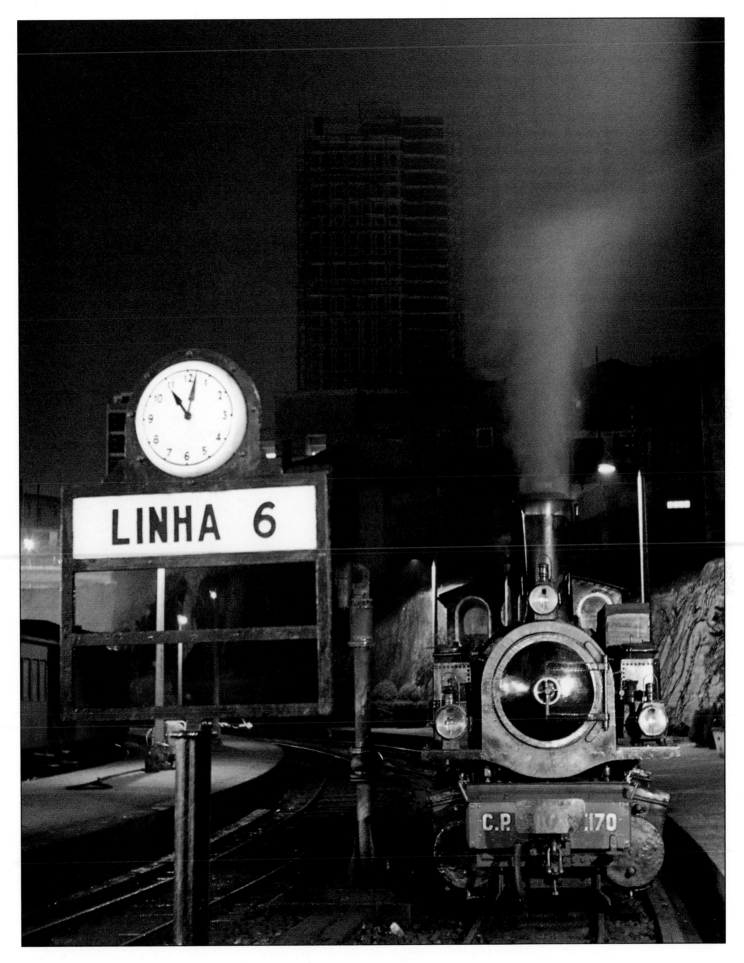

Above: a typical scene in Portugal's Oporto Trindade station, which is the terminus of the metre-gauge routes radiating from the city. Simmering gently against the buffer stops is one of the system's 0-4-4-0T Mallets built in 1908.

Facing page: *Eslava*, one of Spain's ancient outside cylinder 0-6-0s. She was built by Hartmann of Chemnitz in 1881, and is seen here in 1971 ending her days at Ujo colliery. Above: standing at Senhora da Hora, on Oporto's metre-gauge suburban system, is a 2-6-0T (above) built to an 1880s design by Emil Kessler in 1904.

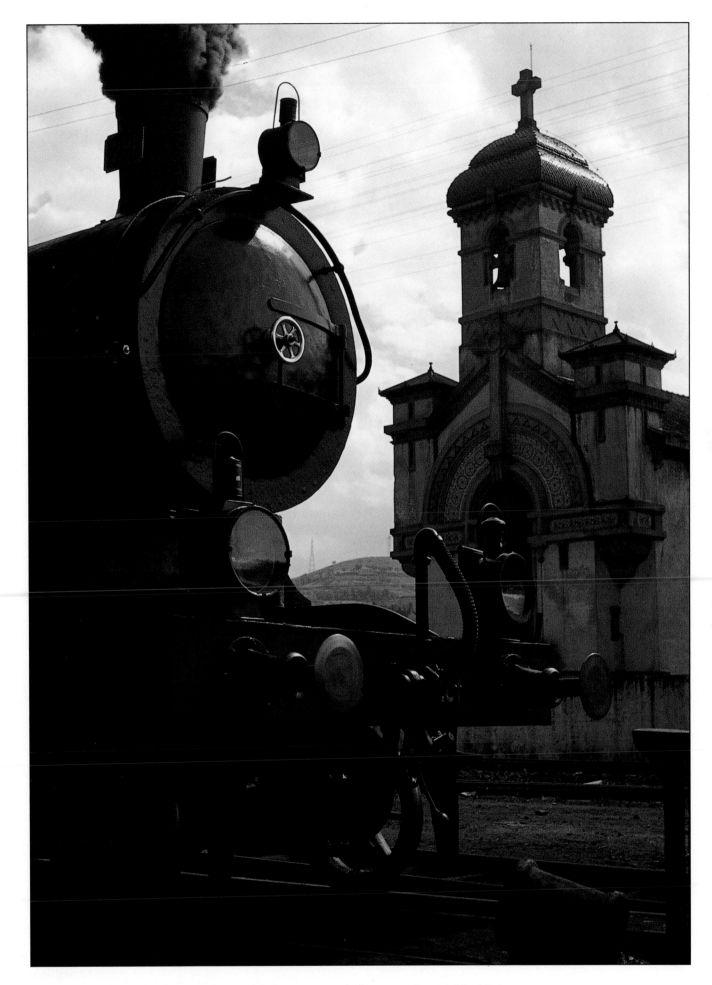

The ultimate Spanish locomotives for the 5ft 6in gauge main lines were the mighty 4-8-4 Confederations (facing page), ten of which were built by Maquinista of Barcelona during the mid 1950s. Above: blending superbly with the line-side architecture at Regua is one of the Douro Valley's shapely inside cylinder 4-6-0s .

The 4-8-0 type was widely used in Spain, where weight restrictions and curves abounded on many lines. Shown (above) is one of these engines boiling up at Salamanca. Facing page: one of the Portuguese Railway's magnificent four-cylinder compound 2-8-0s, first introduced in 1912, at work on the Douro Valley line.

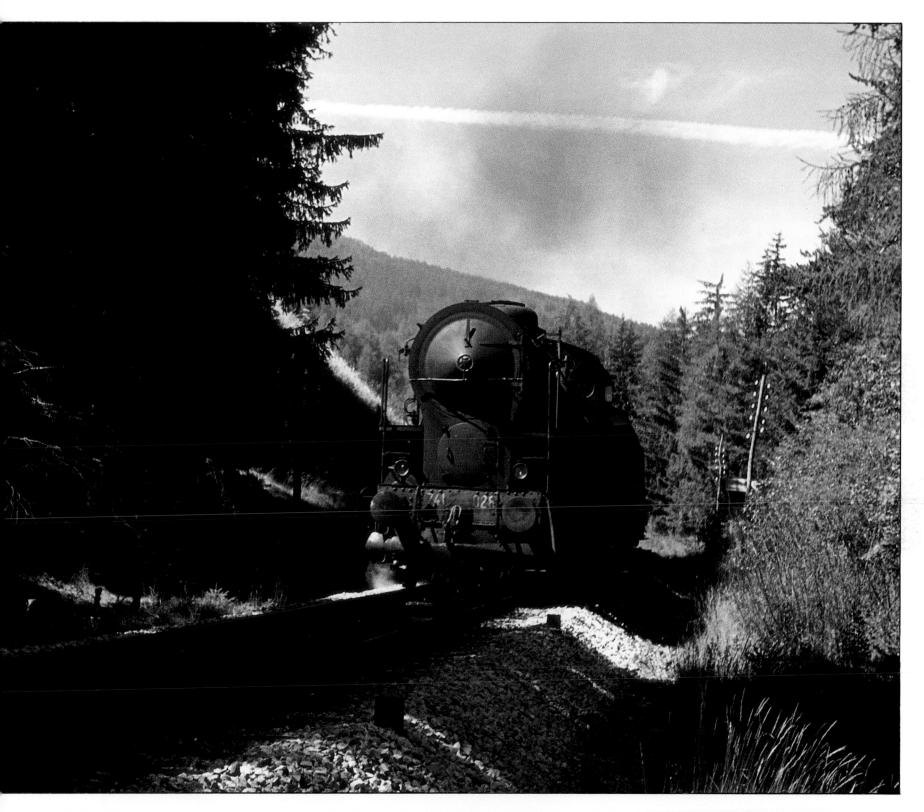

The 740 Class 2-8-0 was a standard freight design on Italian Railways for some sixty years and was the country's most numerous class. They survived until the end of regular steam working, and even today one hears occasional reports of 740s being turned out for pilot and ballasting work. Left: a 740 passing through Cornuda with a Belluno-Treviso freight. The 740 Class was one of the types chosen by Italian Railways to be rebuilt with Crosti boilers. This marvellous innovation was a pre-heater drum slung beneath the normal boiler to convey the hot gases from the smokebox in order to heat the feed water. This resulted in the chimney being placed at the firebox end of the locomotive. The modified engines were reclassified 741, and some eighty examples were so modified during the 1950s. Above: a 741 drawing a passenger train along the Fortessa to San Candido line in the northern part of the country.

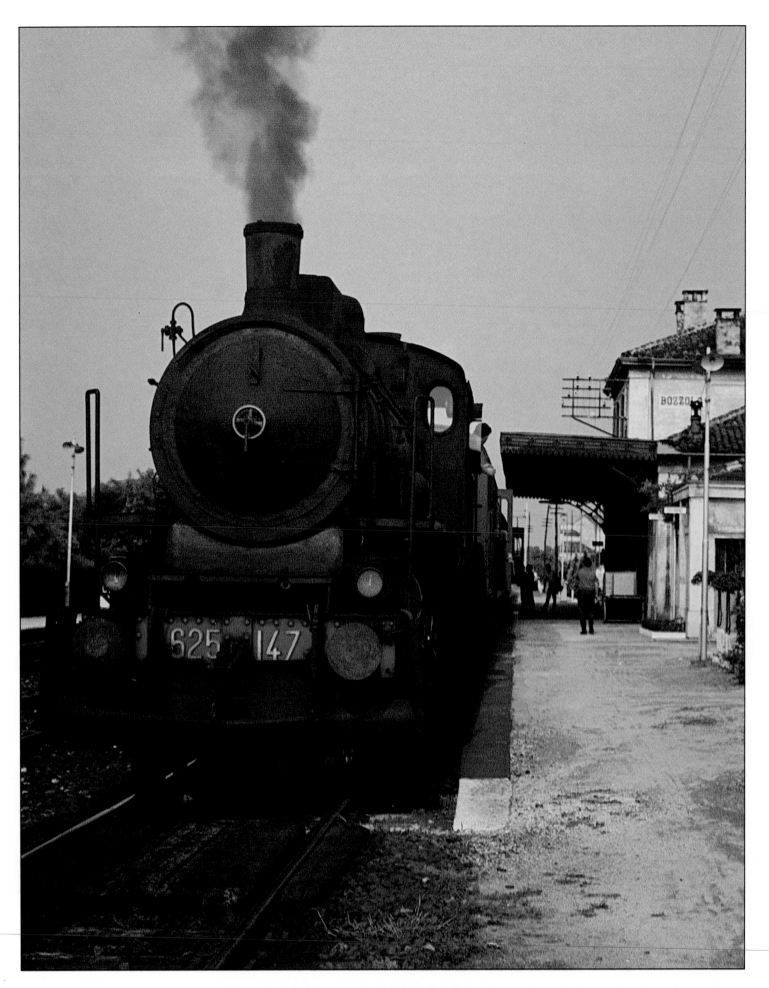

In the early '70s, Italy operated about 1,000 steam locomotives. Most were standard classes whose origin could be traced back to the nationalisation of Italy's railways in 1905. One of the stalwart designs to emerge was the 625 Class 2-6-0 Mogul (these pages). They were typically Italian in appearance, with a delightful vintage look, and were to be found on many secondary lines across the country until the end of regular steam working.

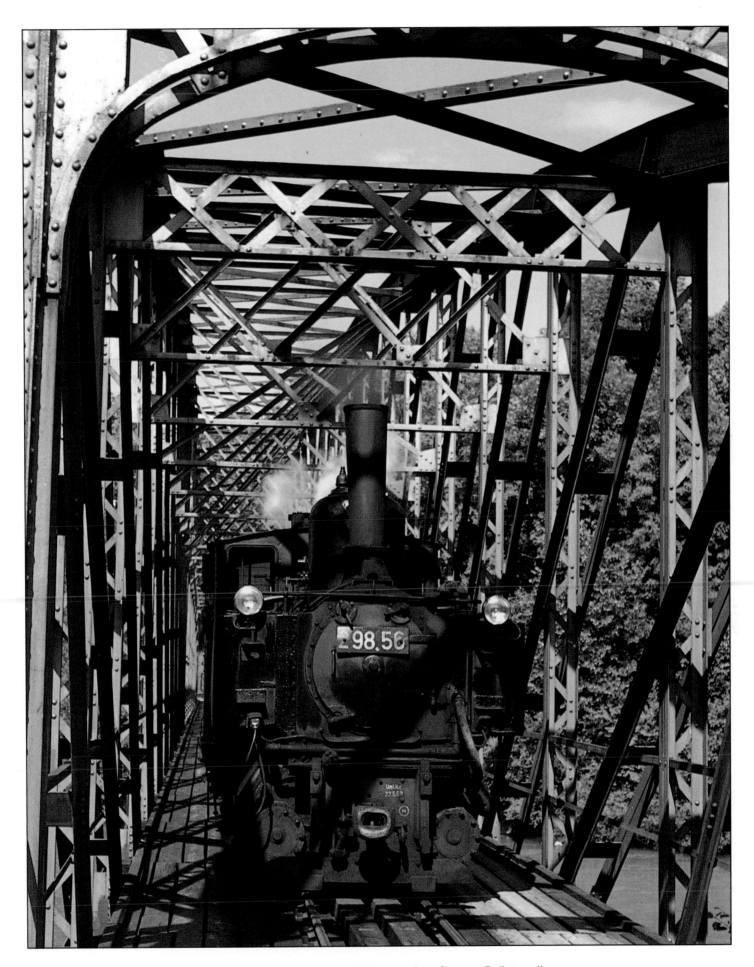

The 50 Class 2-10-0 (facing page) was one of the principal designs used on German Railways. It first appeared in 1938 and over 3,000 were constructed, forming the basis for the German Kriegslokomotive of World War II. Over 6,000 were ultimately built, making the basic design of the mixed traffic 2-10-0 one of the leading locomotive types in world history. Above: an Austrian State Railway narrow-gauge 298 Class crosses the viaduct at Waldrenkirchen, on the Garsten to Molln line.

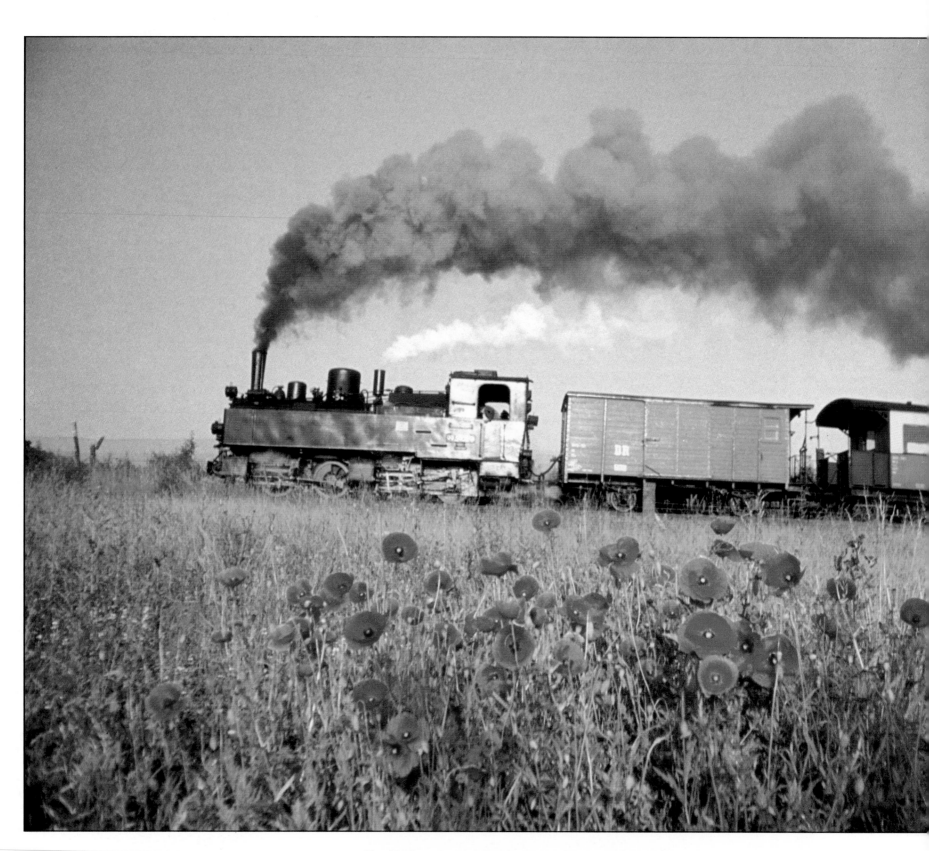

The 25-kilometre-long Selketalbahn runs amid the scenic beauty of the Harz Mountains and is possibly the most delightful of all the German Democractic Republic's narrow-gauge lines. Built to a gauge of one metre, it is traversed by the last Mallets working in the country; they are 0-4-4-Ts and date from the early years of the century. The line begins at Gernrode and runs to a junction at Alexisbad, where it splits; one section climbing up to Harzgerode and the other heading through lush meadowland to Strassberg. Above and right: 0-4-4-Ts departing from Gernrode early in the morning and heading through the flower-strewn countryside with trains bound for Alexisbad.

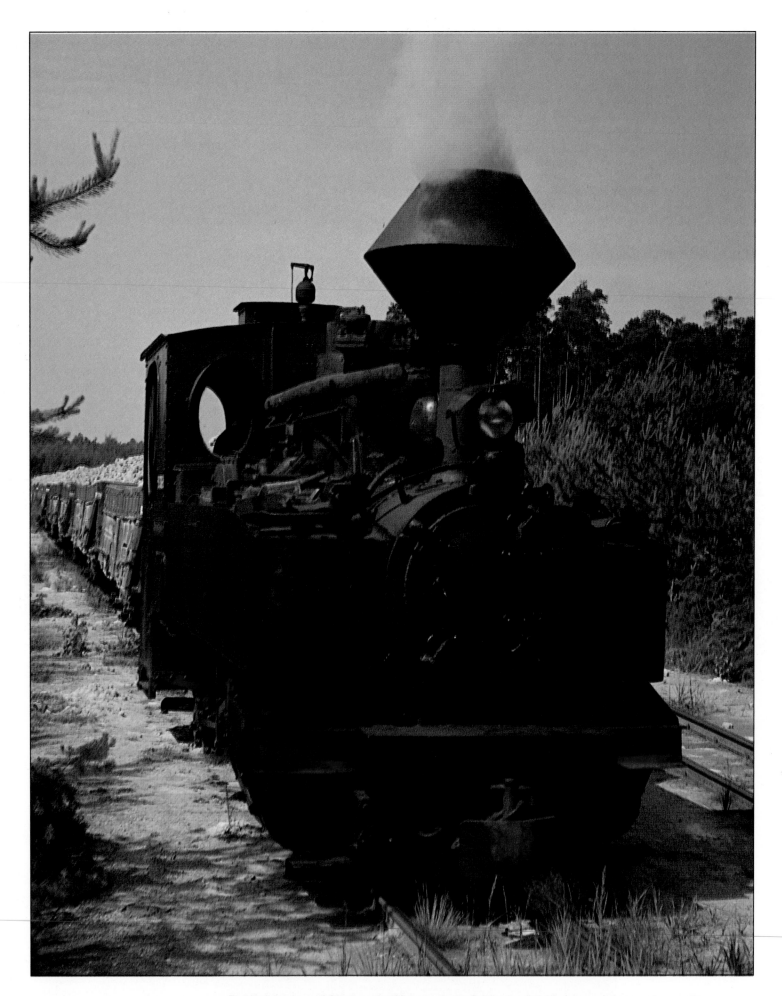

The last survivor of Germany's 600mm-gauge Feldbahn 0-8-0Ts (above) lingered on a clay-carrying railway at Bad Muskau until the late 1970s. Facing page: one of the 0-4-4-0 Mallets on the East German metre-gauge Selketalbahn prepares to leave Silberhutte Station with the 1.44pm train to Strassberg.

Above: two of the exhibits at the narrow-gauge railway museum at Wenecja, in Poland. The engine on the right is of tremendous historical significance: it was the forerunner of the famous Feldbahn engines of World War I, having been built by Orenstein and Koppel in 1911. Right: the last surviving Feldbahn 0-8-0T on the forestry system at Czarna Bialystok, alongside the Russian border in northeastern Poland. Several thousand Feldbahns were built to follow the German armies all over Europe during the First World War. After the war they were surplus to military requirements and many gravitated to forestry and industrial railways.

Left: two classic European designs boil up side by side in Slovenia. On the left is one of the German Kriegslokomotive 2-10-0s, some of which passed to Yugoslavia as reparations following World War II, and on the right a 28 Class Austrian State Railway 0-10-0, many of which were ceded to Yugoslavia upon its creation as a separate nation following World War I. One of the largest and most important of the Hungarian State Railway designs was the 424 Class 4-8-0 (above). This type also saw prolific service in Yugoslavia, for whom examples were built in Budapest until the mid 1950s. They formed the Yugoslav State Railway's 11 Class.

Watching these magnificent 0-10-0s (these pages) working over the hill lines of Slovenia with their heavy freights was a memorable experience. The type is descended from the 180 Class two-cylinder compound 0-10-0s of 1900, designed by the legendary Austrian engineer Karl Golsdorf. When rebuilt as simples with superheaters, they were reclassified 80.9 and the type performed magnificently on the sinuous routes throughout Austria. On the Yugoslav State Railway they were known as the 28 Class. Above: one of them prepares to take water at Stanjel, a village of Roman origin, whilst heading a Nova Gorica to Sezana freight. The locomotive dates from the Austrian Empire, and the track was cast by Krupp of Germany during the 19th century. Right: a Yugoslav State Railway 51 Class 2-6-2T heads a morning freight from Karlovac to Sisak.

Yugoslavia's 51 Class 2-6-2Ts (these pages) represent one of the most remarkable survivors in Europe. Originally the Hungarian State Railway Class 375, the first examples of the 51 Class appeared in 1907. They were important among several branch line types designed for the lightly laid rural lines of the territory and, despite their archaic appearance, they continued to be built in Hungary until 1959. Yugoslavia inherited them from Croatia, which was formerly Hungarian territory, and fifteen were built at Yugoslavia's Slavonksi Brod works in 1942. The stud currently active on the Karlovac to Sisak line includes both original Hungarian and Yugoslavian engines. Above: the overnight passenger train from Karlovac to Sisak during its long wait at Vrginmost.

Italy, devoid of coalfields, needed to conserve energy as effectively as possible, and this gave rise to the rebuilding of standard 740 Class 2-8-0s into the Franco Crosti boilered 743 Class (above). This was a gallant attempt to utilise the hot gases more fully by feeding them back through two large pre-heater drums containing the boiler feed water, and exhausting them at the locomotive's firebox end at a much lower temperature than on a conventional locomotive. This Italian innovation spread to a number of other countries during the later years of steam development, and savings in coal consumption of up to ten per cent were reported. The Hungarian Railway's 324 Class Prairie 2-6-2 was first introduced in 1909. They were superb engines for middle range duties and were widely used in Yugoslavia as the 22 Class. Right: the last survivor at Varazdin shortly before she was towed to the breaker's yard at Zapresic, on the outskirts of nearby Zagreb.

Turkey has achieved much recognition over the last decade for retaining a wide variety of standard gauge designs descended from German, British and American builders. The Turkish State Railways have been intent upon dieselisation for many years, but have never been able to implement the programme as scheduled and to this day, an ever dwindling variety of steam designs can still be found in the country. Top left: a fine contrast in motive power at the EKI colliery exchange sidings in Catalagzi, in Zonguldak on the Black Sea coast. On the left is a former Turkish Railways 0-6-0T, which now belongs to the colliery for shunting the exchange sidings. On the right is one of the colliery's metre-gauge 0-6-0 pannier tanks, built by Bagnalls of Stafford in 1942. The two shed pilots (left) at Irmak junction are highly distinctive designs. On the left is an ex Prussian G82 Class 2-8-0 and on the right, one of the celebrated Stanier 8F 2-8-0s which passed to Turkey following World War II. Above: a magnificently trimmed example of a Turkish State Railway German Kriegslokomotive, complete with the Turkish state emblem on its cab side.

The busy suburban services around the Agean port of Izmir were worked by a marvellous range of veteran locomotives, amongst them the Prussian G8 0-8-0s. One of the most numerous locomotive designs in history, the G8s eventually totalled 5,200 engines. Their distribution was widespread, especially as a result of the turmoil caused by two world wars, and their subsequent territorial changes and reparations. It is marvellous that, seventy years after the inception of the class in 1913, this Prussian freight engine (above) should still be working passenger trains around a modern Turkish city. Right: a rare example of French design, built by Humbolt of Paris in 1912 for Turkey's Smyrna Cassaba and Prolonguements Railway, is seen here waiting in Izmir to take an evening train to Buca.

This powerful Turkish Railways two-cylinder 2-8-0 (above) was built to the design of the Prussian G82 Class, which once numbered more than 1,000 locomotives – sixty-two being built for Turkey alone between 1927-35. The former LMS Stanier 8F Class 2-8-0 (facing page) was one of Britain's most numerous steam types, of which over 700 examples were built. Many were built during World War II, and twenty examples eventually passed to Turkey, where survivors lingered on, performing secondary duties until well into the 1980s. Overleaf: dawn on the border of the Arctic Circle during a footplate journey on Finnish Railway's TR1 Class 2-8-2 Mikado No. 1074. The engine was working a Rovaniemi to Raajarvi ballast haul and, during the course of the journey, crossed the Arctic Circle into Finnish Lapland.

Finland's highly distinctive designs were among the bright spots in the closing years of steam in Europe and Scandinavia. One of the best-loved designs were the TK3 Class 2-8-0s. The Finns called them 'Little Jumbos', and with an axle loading of only 10.7 tonnes, they were able to work over a wide variety of lines. First introduced in 1927, building continued until 1953, by which time a total of 161 had been constructed, making them Finland's most numerous type. Many were wood burners and were supplied with characteristic spark-arresting chimneys, such as the one on No. 1163 (above) engaged in tripping duties around Rovaniemi. Along with many countries, Finland adopted a standardisation policy based around Mikado 2-8-2s and Pacific 4-6-2s with interchangable boilers. Right: one of their TR1 Class Mikados, which totalled sixty-seven engines. Known as 'Ristos', they were among the last steam locomotives to work in Finland, and many have been mothballed as part of a strategic reserve. Overleaf: as winter relaxes its icy grip upon Finland's rivers, a TV1 Class 2-8-0 ambles towards Kontiomäki with a sand ballast train for permanent way engineers. Introduced in 1917, the TV1 totalled ninety-seven engines when building finished in 1945.

STEAM IN INDIA AND PAKISTAN

Running some 5,000 locomotives, the Indian subcontinent is now the world's second largest bastion of steam traction. With 11,000 examples in service, China is well ahead of this, but their fleet is standardised, containing few locomotives more than fifty years old, whereas the surviving engines on the Indian sub-continent are highly varied and often of great antiquity.

The vastness of Indian railways is hard to appreciate by European standards. In addition to the great distances covered, the network is densely laid and intensively utilised. Roads, such as those known in the West, barely exist, so the railway remains the preferred form of transportation. The building of India's railways was one of the great achievements of the British Empire; most of the extensive system was laid before the end of the Raj, having been financed, designed, engineered, built and operated under British jurisdiction. The railways constructed by those intrepid pioneers extended from Burma to the Khyber Pass and from the Himalayas to Ceylon. The railway unified India industrially and socially, just as the English language unified her culturally. Four gauges eventually came into operation and these created mainline networks of five foot, six inches and metre gauge, alongside many feeder systems and rural railways that adopted a gauge of 2ft, or 2ft 6in.

Imperial locomotive designs for the Indian railways followed those of the old country; indeed, the subcontinent's railways, as they evolved in all their private diversity, resembled the pre-grouping years of Britain's railways. During the nineteenth century, the companies ordered their designs with predictable individualism from Britain, though the building of locomotives in the purest of British traditions had begun at Jamalpur and Ajmer before the turn of the century.

This proliferation of types caused concern, so, in 1905, the British Engineering Standards Association (BESA) designs were prepared. These were intended to fulfil the needs of all the subcontinent's 5ft 6in gauge lines and were comprised of exactly the kind of locomotive then prevalent in Britain: inside-cylinder 0-6-0s, inside-cylinder 4-G-0s, Atlantics, 4-6-0s and 2-8-0s. The BESA standards were exported in large numbers from many of the major British builders and fulfilled their task superbly, but by the 1920s loads were increasing and the narrow fireboxes of the traditional British locomotives were causing increasing difficulties with the poorer standard Indian coal. This led to the next major series of British designs for the subcontinent – the famous X series. These were comprised of three classes of Pacific for light, medium and heavy work, classified XA, XB and XC, and two Mikado 2-8-2s for medium and heavy freight hauls, classified XD and XE respectively. All these classes had wide fire boxes designed to cope with poorer coal, and the series was rounded off by the heavy shunting XF and mighty hump-shunting XG, so necessary for the vast marshalling yards that had grown to keep pace with Indian railway development.

With their wide fireboxes (a design concept derived from America), the X series represented a partial departure from traditional British practice, and the departure was completed during World War II when India took a number of pure American designs, one of which was a 5ft 6in gauge version of the classic S160 2-8-0 supplied by America as aid for Britain and Europe. America also provided the AWE and CWD Class Mikados, which were pure American versions of the XE and XD types. The ruggedness of these bar-framed imports proved ideal for Indian conditions, and thenceforth the subcontinent looked to American traditions for the remainder of her major steam designs. This was made all the easier after 1947 when British rule ceased. India's final choice of broad gauge standards was restricted to two classes: a highly Americanised and partly streamlined Pacific classified WP, which first appeared in 1947, and a closely related Mikado classified WG for heavy freight work, which first appeared in 1950. These designs were built in many countries and, in all, reached a total of more than 3,000 engines.

The world famous Indian variety of engines does not apply to those designed for broad gauge. None of the BESA standards or even the X series remain in line service, although isolated examples from both groups may be found on industrial lines. Even the American incursions from the Second World War have recently been taken out of service, leaving the entire broad gauge network with only WPs and WGs. Both can still be found performing the duties for which they were originally designed, although WPs are increasingly found on secondary stopping trains (jobs which are so low key in performance that they are easily interchangeable with WGs), whilst now WGs are usually relegated to shunting and tripping work.

The varied collection of classic British designs for the metre gauge has also disappeared and services on these networks are now dominated by the YP Pacifics and YG Mikados – the American-influenced counterparts of the WPs and WGs. By far the greatest variety exists on the narrow gauge lines that are not interconnected, which tend to retain their original form of individualistic motive power wherever steam traction survives. The most famous of these is the Darjeeling and Himalayan Railway, which climbs 7,407 feet to the former British summer resort boasting commanding views of the snow-capped Himalayas. The charm and rusticity of these systems is unequalled anywhere in the world and eloquently mirrors the heyday of the rural railway in Britain; here copper-capped antiquities whose spiritual home lies in the soft English countryside still play a vital role in the rural economy of developing India.

Right: a British-built inside cylinder 0-6-0 from the BESA period approaches Dandot, in the Pakistan Punjab. Similar engines were used on the 5ft 6in gauge lines of the Indian subcontinent, from the Khyber Pass to Bangladesh.

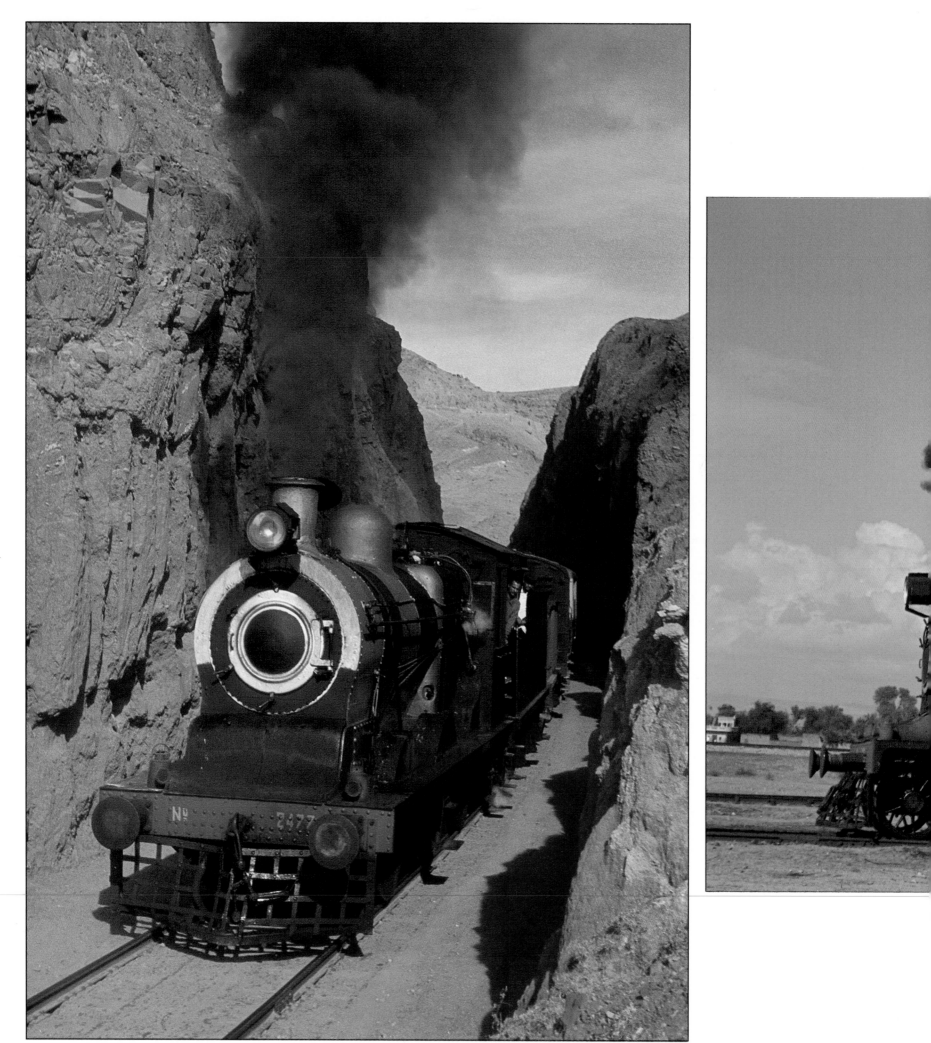

A great variety of types is also to be found on India's industrial lines, and many of these are ex-mainliners, including some nineteenth-century examples from small, regionally based systems dating back to the very beginning of railway development in India. A perfect example is the once ubiquitous F Class 0-6-Q; this locomotive was built in vast numbers as a metre gauge standard design from the 1870s until the 1920s, and is recognised today as one of the classics of world locomotive history.

In absolute contrast, neighbouring Pakistan has relatively few narrow gauge lines and a somewhat limited metre gauge system. It is the country's 5ft 6in gauge lines that have bought it world renown, as here two of the most important types in the BESA standard series – amazingly and against all odds – remain hard at work. These are the inside cylinder 0-6-0 and related inside cylinder 4-4-0 – the definitive freight and express passenger types of late-Victorian Britain.

The two principal forms of British locomotive during the late 19th century were the inside cylinder 0-6-0, for heavy freight and mixed traffic duties, and the closely related inside cylinder 4-4-0, for express passenger duties. Most of Britain's privately owned railway companies possessed both types, often fitted with interchangeable boilers. During these years there were enormous exports of locomotives to British India, and almost identical designs were prepared for the subcontinent under the BESA scheme at the beginning of the 20th century. It is incredible that today, more than eighty years later, examples of these definitive Victorian 0-6-0s and 4-4-0s remain in evidence on the railways of Pakistan. The principal centre is the cross-country junction of Malakal, in the Punjab. All are now oil-burning, since Pakistan has no coal fields. Left: an inside cylinder 0-6-0 heads away from Malakal as a gracefully-shaped inside cylinder 4-4-0 (above) boils up in the depot yard.

Many British classics were exported to India under the X series standardisation scheme of the 1920s, notably the beautiful XC Class Pacific (above), and the XD Class 2-8-2 Mikado (right). The XCs have a typical 1920s appearance and were the last greyhounds of British steam to remain in world service. The class totalled seventy-two engines, which came primarily from the Vulcan Foundry at Newton-le-Willows in Lancashire, although the final twelve came from the legendary Clyde shipbuilding firm of Beardsmore during the early '30s. The XD Class 2-8-2 Mikado was a powerful heavy freight and mixed traffic design, first introduced from the Vulcan Foundry in 1927. When building finished in 1948, the class totalled almost 200 engines. They were well regarded, bearing, as they did, all the elements of traditional British craftsmanship. XDs were operating 1,800-tonne trains over the seventy-seven miles from Dornakal Junction to Vijaywada until the 1960s, completing the journey in two-and-a-quarter hours – enduring proof that the steam locomotive is not an outmoded relic. Overleaf: HSM Class 2-8-0 No. 26190 takes us back to the BESA period. She was built for the Bengal and Nagpur Railway by Armstrong Whitworth of Newcastle-upon-Tyne in 1924. These handsome British 2-8-0s ended their days working empty stock trains around Calcutta.

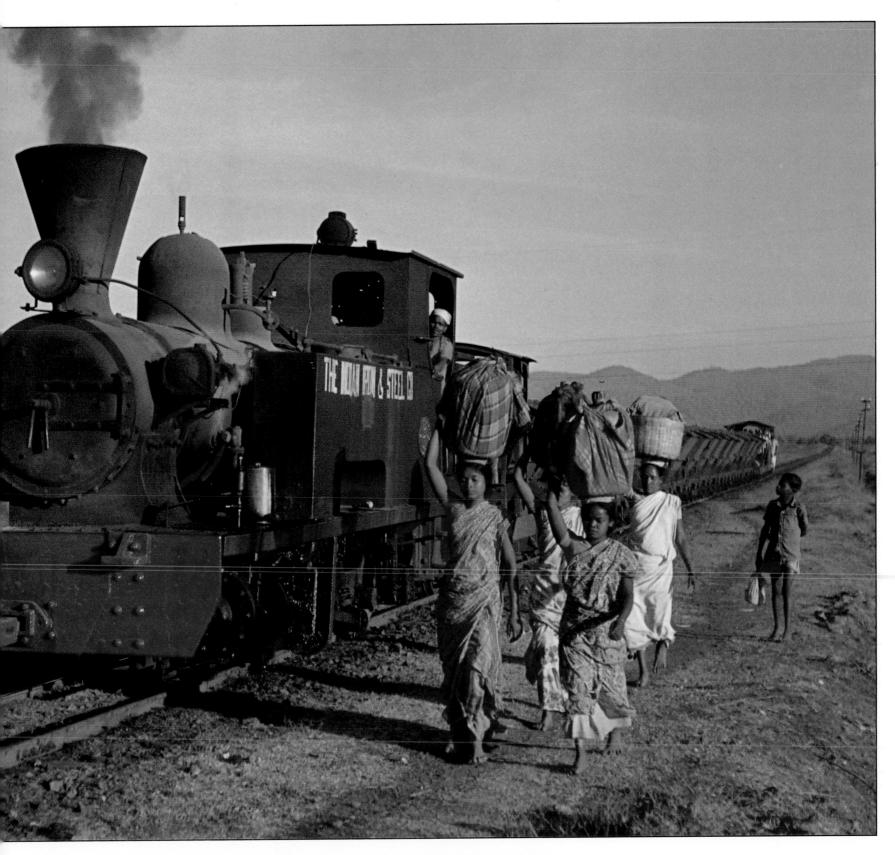

For many years, railway operations around Calcutta's vast docks were performed by these heavy duty 0-6-2 side tanks (left and top left), which first came from Hunslet's Leeds works in 1945. Having found the type satisfactory, the Calcutta Port Trust – unlike most industrial steam users – decided to standardise its locomotive fleet around one design. Accordingly, when further locomotives were needed, the Calcutta Port Trust insisted on the same design. That notwithstanding, the second batch came from Henschel of Germany, and the final batch from Mitsubishi of Japan in 1954. Above: an Indian Iron and Steel Corporation Andrew Barclay built 0-4-2T heads a loaded iron-ore train to the South Eastern Railway's connection at Manoharpur.

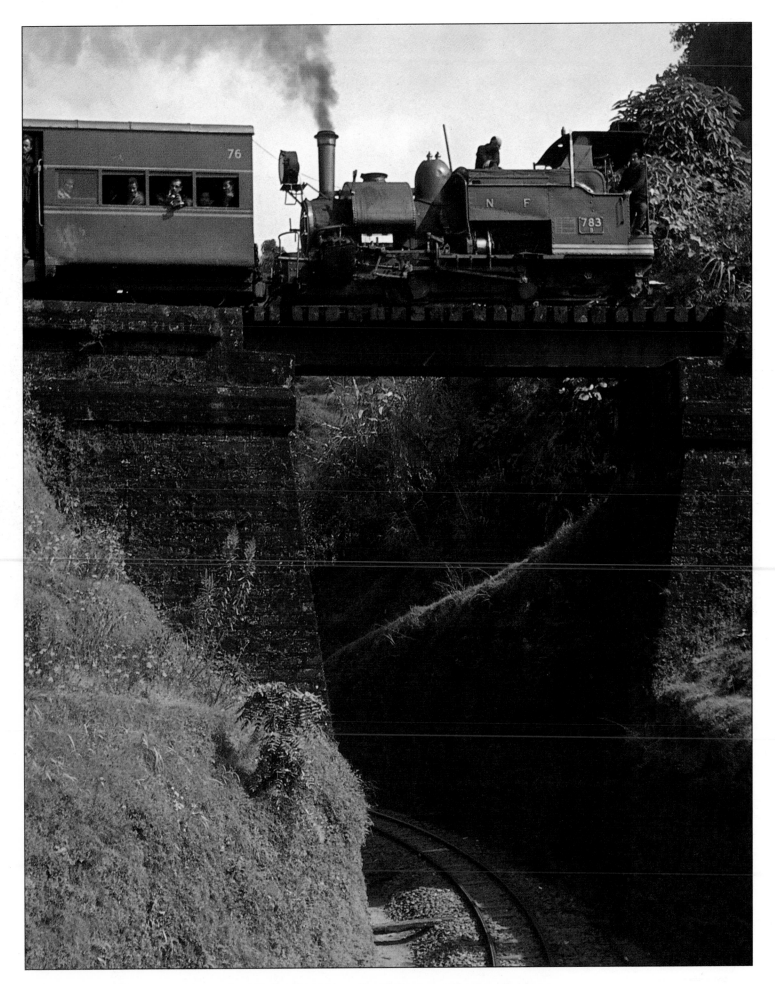

Facing page: a 0-6-4T, built by Bagnalls of Stafford in 1914, on the 2ft 6in gauge line from Burdwan to Katwa. Above: the world-famous Darjeeling-Himalayan Railway, which climbs 7,400 feet during its fifty-five mile journey to the former British summer resort. Overleaf: one of the last surviving Indian Railway XD Class 2-8-2s.

The British sailed from Calcutta in Scottish-built paddle steamers and plied their way up the rivers of what is now Bangladesh to enter the great Brahmaputra River, from there to sail eastwards and enter the dense, inhospitable and leech-ridden jungles of Assam. Once there, the intrepid pioneers developed many industries: logging, tea planting and coal mining. It was perhaps inevitable that Staffordshire-built saddle tanks should follow their enterprise and today, almost a century later, some still survive. *David* (above) worked at Tirap colliery close to the Burmese border, coming originally from Bagnall's Castle Engine Works in Stafford in 1924. Left: *Sally*, a Bagnall engine of 1930. These engines were supplied to the Assam Railways and Trading Company, the organisation established by the British to develop the wealth of Upper Assam. The 0-6-0 crane tank (facing page) was exported from Manning Wardle's works in Leeds in 1903. Her crane structure and the auxiliary engine which drives it came from Joseph Booth and Sons, who were located in the Leeds suburb of Rodley. She worked at an Indian sleeper depot and part of her duty was to lift tree trunks and convey them to the sawmill to be cut into sleeper lengths for use on Indian Railway's main lines.

A pair of Fireless engines (top left) work at the Ludlow Jute Mill on the banks of the Hooghley River, Calcutta. They are both 0-4-0s from Orenstein and Koppel, but of very different design. Both have their feed valves located at the front, but the engine on the left has its cylinders and chimney to the rear, whilst the right-hand engine has conventionally-placed cylinders and chimney. The veteran 0-4-2 well tank (left) is possibly the last survivor from Dick Kerr's Britannia works in Kilmarnock, Scotland. She was originally built for the Karachi Port Trust, but ended her days working at the Dhilwan creosoting plant in India's Punjab. Above: *Cheetal*, a delightful 0-6-0 well tank built by John Fowler's works, Leeds, in 1923, heads along the 2ft gauge metals of the Upper India Sugar Mills with a loaded train. Overleaf: one of Ludlow Jute Mills' Fireless engines, having taken a fresh charge of steam from the factory boilers, eases along the jetty with a loaded train.

STEAM IN CHINA

Over recent years China has received international fame for her steam railways. The media throughout the Western world has reported the fact that China continues to build steam locomotives – news which amazed enthusiasts and laymen alike. With 11,000 steam locomotives in service, China is now synonymous with the age of steam. The country is vast, contains one quarter of the world's population and has become a powerful, industrialised nation largely dependent upon public transport. Given this situation, it is not difficult to imagine the density of operations throughout China's enormous railway network.

Before China's opening up to the West, it was popularly believed that the country was host to all kinds of exotic rarities, but the opposite proved to be the case. Standardisation has been rigorously pursued, both before and especially since the founding of the People's Republic – only Russia has ever approached such a remarkable degree of standardisation. Of the 11,000 locomotives at work, some 9,000 can be accounted for by six basic types. Topping the list are the QJ Class Advanced Forward 2-10-2s, with over 4,000 believed to be in service. These handle the heaviest freightwork, aided by the smaller JS Class construction 2-10-2s of which there are some 1,500 in service. The JSs are based on an earlier, Mikado-classified JF of which around 1,000 remain at work, whilst slightly smaller is the SY Class Aiming High Industrial Mikado with another 1,500 in service. Only two passenger classes exist and both are Pacifics: the SL6, which dates back to the 1930s, and the more recent RM Class, which between them account for another 1,000 locomotives.

Though heavily standardised, China's railways present the enthusiast with incomparable spectacles. Nowhere else can busy main lines be found which are almost a hundred percent steam operated on which trains pass every twenty minutes or so day and night. A typical line may see QJs on the long-distance freights, a few JSs on pick-up freights, and perhaps one of the Pacific classes on certain passenger turns, although other equally busy lines may only see QJs. The density of activity and full-blooded action more than offsets the lack of variety, but, in any case, the locomotives within any given class vary greatly, if not in mechanical details, then in terms of embellishments, which in China take on a fascinating diversity and provide a constant source of interest.

In view of the massive world publicity about China's steam railways, it is sometimes supposed that the country has an outright steam policy, but many main lines are electrified and this form of traction proceeds apace as, indeed, does dieselisation. Many of China's long-distance express trains were dieselised years ago and the remainder are rapidly being converted, partly because the increasingly heavy weights are beyond the capacity of the Pacifics. Despite China's avid modernisation programme, the steam total has fluctuated remarkably little. This is a unique situation brought about by two basic factors. The first stems from the fact that the country's economy is developing rapidly, leading to a massive increase in rail traffic – new locomotives merely cope with the increase instead of eroding the steam total. The second factor is that China continues to build new railways, many of them important long-distant routes, and as these tend to use modern traction from the outset, they are another area of demand for all the diesels and electrics that China can either build or import. Equally important, though, is the fact that when some of the non-standard and even older examples of the standard classes are withdrawn, they have been replaced by newly built examples of classes QJ, JS and SY.

Throughout history, the Chinese have been attributed with great wisdom and certainly their policy of utilising whatever form of traction is most appropriate for a particular circumstance has been refreshingly clear in its thinking. The country is rich in coal and iron reserves and also has an abundance of labour. Given these factors in a centralised socialist economy, it makes good sense to use steam traction.

So vast and exciting are China's main lines that many of the country's industrial and narrow gauge systems have tended to be overlooked. In the case of collieries and iron and steel works, the standard SY Mikado has now all but replaced the fascinating array of former mainline types that survived in these environments until recent years, but the narrow gauge systems see a completely different range of motive power, although even here standardisation is remarkably advanced. Of the country's forestry lines, 762 millimetre gauge 0-8-0s, built to a basic standard design, predominate over many systems, particularly in the northeastern province of Heilongjiang. Descended from a Russian engine, isolated examples of this type continue to be built at the Harbin Forest Machinery Company's works. Far more extensive than these systems, however, are China's local railways; these are also built to 762 millimetre gauge and operated by provincial or local governments to provide public passenger and freight services in rural areas. In Henan and Hebei provinces alone, these local railways have 1,550 miles of route in operation. Many are worked by steam, although diesels are encroaching, but whatever form of motive power is used, it has recently been reported that the average cost per route mile of these local lines is between a third and a half of the cost of road transport. As with China's burgeoning main lines, construction of local railways continues and it is anticipated that by the end of the century some 10,000 route miles could be in operation.

So China is the country of steam, but equally importantly and perhaps more accurately, she is the country of railways – perhaps the last truly railway-based economy on earth. One fears that as Western commerical influences exert ever greater pressures on China as part of her opening-up policy, this situation may change and the idea of road development begin to take hold. However, if this does happen, it will be a long way into the future; for the time being, China's railways still fulfil their purpose throughout the nation, and in so doing provide a stable and secure base for steam traction into the forseeable future.

Facing page: on a misty morning at Harbin, in winter temperatures of -35°C, a QJ Class 2-10-2 pulls up to the water column during routine servicing.

The pride of Harbin is QJ Class 2-10-2 No. 2470 *Zhou De* (these pages). She is one of the best-kept locomotives on China Railways and has been a Harbin engine for many years. Zhou De was one of China's ten marshalls and the man who led the Red Army from its formation in 1927 through the revolution of 1949, when he was second only to Mao himself. Before the founding of the People's Republic of China in 1949, the Red Army was known as the 'Zhou De Mao Army.' Above: with its mechanical stoker activated, *Zhou De* approaches the summit of Wang Gang Bank at the head of a heavy southbound freight. Right: General Zhou De stares impassively from the smokebox of QJ Class No. 2470 as she waits to leave Sankong yard in Harbin. Overleaf: a long rake of oil wagons heads southwards from Anshan behind a QJ Class 2-10-2 bound for the Yellow Sea port of Daliam.

Harbin is known as China's coldest city. The biting Manchurian wind blows in vicious, stinging blasts in temperatures so low that it is almost impossible to control a camera. A pair of QJs (facing page) receive the all clear from Sankong yard and, with chime whistles ringing and mechanical stokers activated, they ease their 2,000-tonne wood train forward. Above: two QJ Class 2-10-2s make a vigorous assault on Wang Gang Bank at the head of a half-mile-long southbound freight. Right: the amplified voice of the yard controller directing operations at Sankong is momentarily drowned by the departure of two QJs with a heavy southbound freight. Overleaf: the big freeze of the Manchurian winter is so severe that it deposits thick layers of ice on all but the very hottest parts of the locomotives.

The YJ Class industrial 2-6-2 Prairie (left) clearly reveals her American ancestry. The YJs are descended from, and almost identical to, the earlier PL2 Class, first introduced in 1941. The JF was for many years a principal freight hauler on many of China's main lines but, with the advent of the JS and QJ classes, they were relegated to secondary work, primarily shunting, tripping and freight-transfer work between marshalling yards. Engine No. 2422 (above) has for many years been the shed pilot at Changchun. She is immediately recognisable by her tender, cut down to facilitate movement of dead engines onto the turntable and into the various bays of the semi-round house. Overleaf: the driver of industrial YJ Class Priarie 2-6-2 No. 290 watches the camera impassively as he waits for the heavy cauldrons to be filled with molten steel at Anshan.

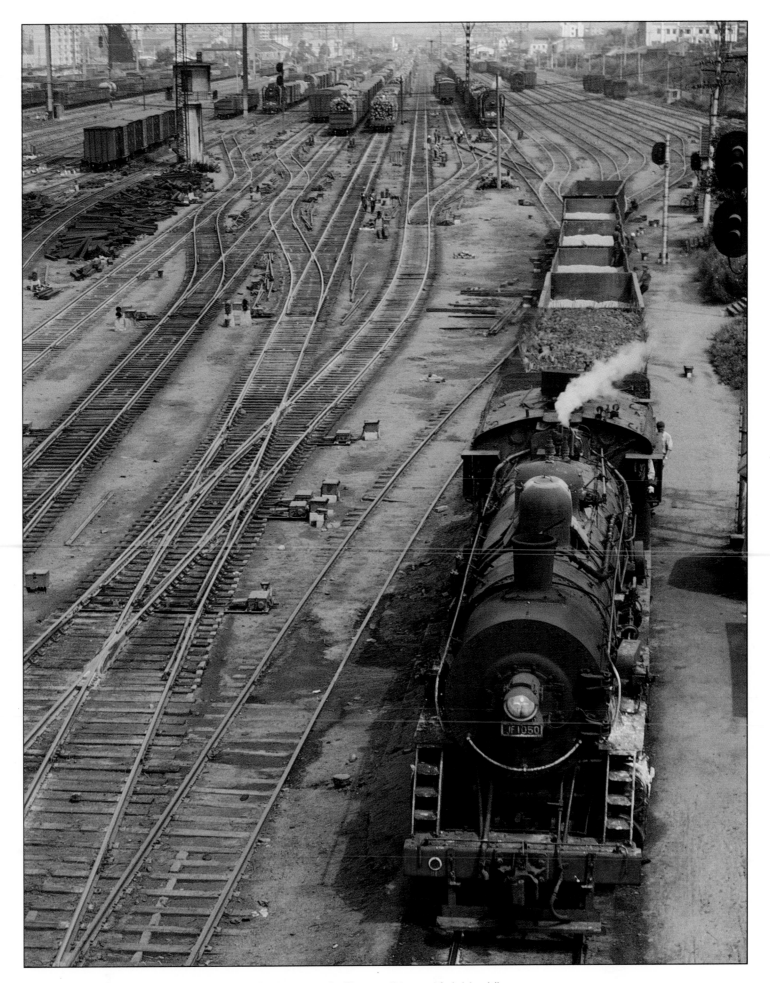

Facing page: a QJ prepares to depart from Sankong yard with a southbound freight, while (above) a JF Class rolls a string of wagons down the hump in readiness for making up the next trains. Overleaf: the magic of the steam age captured in a glorious view of the Sangkong yard.

OVERHAULING AND BUILDING

One of the most exciting experiences in railway history was to visit a huge works to see locomotives of many kinds receiving major overhauls and others being built. Until recently, this was a common sight in many of Britain's railway works which, since pre-grouping times, have overhauled and built locomotives simultaneously. These works often incorporated carriage and wagon shops too, and gave rise to the great railway towns – the legendary names of Crewe, Doncaster, Swindon and Derby immediately spring to mind. The fascination of such operations could not be so readily enjoyed in other railway-building nations, for the policy in many countries was for railway companies to order their new locomotives from private builders and be responsible only for overhauling and maintaining their fleets. In Britain, too, railway companies have frequently ordered from the private sector, but this has invariably been due to their incapacity to produce the required locomotives quickly enough in their own works.

The overhauling of a locomotive may be split into two principal areas. The first, the routine servicing and maintainance, is carried out at the locomotive's home depot. This work involves such matters as boiler washouts and the replacement of valves and pistons, bearings and other relatively simple components that have failed. The other aspect of overhauling concerns major structural work for which the locomotive is sent to the builder's yard, usually to be completely stripped down to its frame for detailed attention to such heavy components as its boiler and firebox, frame, cylinders, wheels and tyres . Most steam locomotives need a major overhaul of this kind every three years after a certain mileage has been reached, and so it is a common sight on a steam railway to see grimy, work-weary engines plodding their way towards the shops, only to return some two months later freshly painted, running almost noiselessly and, to all intents and purposes, appearing as new.

The steam age having long since vanished from much of the Western world, it is remarkable to think that building in Britain only ended as recently as 1960. Within eight years the steam age in that country had ended, and large numbers of locomotives were sent to breakers' yards after a working life of only a few years. Building in other developed countries had finished some years before this, and Britain was noteworthy in being one of the first to build, yet one of the last to annihilate, steam traction. After this, only India and China pursued a building policy, the former continuing to produce WPs and WGs from their Chittaranjan works in Bengal until the mid 1970s. This left China as the only country with a prolonged building policy, a situation that continued throughout the 1980s as the Datong works in Shanxi Province produced both JS Class Mikados and QJ Class 2-10-2s and, in far-away Tangshan in Hebei Province, production of the industrial SY Class Mikado proceeds apace.

Operations at Datong were actually as enthusiastic as any in railway history; the works did not open until 1959, but since then it has produced over 4,000 QJs and the maximum number produced in any month was thirty – exactly one a day. In twenty-five years, Datong built more than half the total of locomotives produced by Crewe in more than a century; however, Datong, in common with Tangshan, is merely a production plant and no overhauling activities are undertaken there. Only in 1989 did news come of any significant change in Chinese policy, when it was declared that Datong had finally ceased to build and that operations at Tangshan were being scaled down. Despite this, steam building in China will go into the 1990s. When it finally ceases, it will close an incredible chapter of industrial world history that spanned almost two centuries.

Changchun locomotive works (above) is one of the largest in China, employing 5,000 people and completing some 300 major overhauls a year. It is responsible for locomotives from the Harbin, Changchun and Jilin areas and handles four principal classes: QJs, JSs, RMs and SL6s, in addition to occasional industrial engines of various gauges.

The Changchun works (these pages and overleaf) is solely responsible for overhauling steam locomotives, although, following its opening in 1958, some early QJs were built there. QJs are sent here for major overhauls after they have run some 300,000 kilometres, and the Changchun works prides itself in turning engines round very quickly, with average overhauls taking less than three weeks. The Chinese may not have been able to improve the steam locomotive's low thermal efficiency, but their avid standardisation programme, intensely utilised diagrams, and carefully zoned overhauling facilities, have produced some of the most impressive utilisation performances in the history of steam traction.

Datong locomotive works (these pages), located in the north of Shanxi Province, on the border with Inner Mongolia, was the last major plant in the world to produce steam locomotives. Since it opened in 1959 it has produced over 4,000 QJs, in addition to various batches of JS Class engines. The works covers half a square mile and employs 8,000 people. Most of the workers live within the complex, which is essentially a separate community. Entering the huge erecting shop and watching the mighty components of the QJs falling into place was an unforgettable experience. It was the sight which, throughout its closing years, attracted people from all parts of the world, and the activities were made doubly exciting when one realised that these last steam giants would almost certainly still be at work in the 21st century.

Above: lines of freshly-painted wheels, with their steel tyres firmly shrunk into place, wait to be rolled beneath the giants in readiness for towing to the adjacent steam testing sheds. Having satisfactorily passed all its steam tests and undertaken its high speed runs on the nearby test track, QJ Class 2-10-2 No. 6979 (right) has had its flamingo works undercoat replaced by standard black livery and is ready to take its place on the world's most rapidly expanding railway network. Any embellishments and adornments will be supplied once the engine enters regular service from its home shed. Overleaf: a brace of QJs, glistening in their flamingo works undercoats, stand in light steam within Datong's gloomy steam testing shed. Each new engine is steam tested for several days, and during this time it will make several runs at high speed light engine along the adjacent test track.

Above: the twice-weekly mixed train from Tabora to Mpanda in Tanzania heads gingerly along the lightly laid track behind No. 2611, a British-built Mikado which came from the Vulcan Foundry in 1952. Her traditional British shape is somewhat marred by the addition of a Giesl chimney, feed water heater, Westinghouse pump and air cylinders. She is the last survivor of the former Tanganyika Railway's ML Class and was specially retained for this line on account of her nine-and-three-quarter-tonne axle load. In addition to serving a Russian gold mine at Mpanda, this line is also important for the delivery of water to remote tribes during the dry season.

Africa is intricately laced with railways, and Cecil Rhodes's dream for a route from the Cape to Cairo could and should have become a reality long ago. Railway development in Africa was closely associated with Britain through her Imperial, commercial and military activities. The exploits of British engineers, as they built railways across this dark and largely undiscovered continent, are among the great legends of the railway age. Indeed, railways opened up Africa as they did North America, although the difficulties of utilising and sustaining so alien a form of technology in an under-industrialised continent with many national boundaries and a proliferation of languages and cultures remains a problem to the present day.

The forging of railways on such a continent was a daunting task financially, so costs were kept to a minimum and from the outset narrow gauge lines were chosen and laid on track beds which were, of necessity, lightly laid with heavy curvature and steep gradients. This contrasted with the railways of the developed world that had been built to a larger gauge on firmer and more consistent foundations. Yet the limitations imposed by the narrow gauge were partly offset by the building of locomotives that were proportionally larger than those running on the standard gauge networks.

The continent's locomotives ranged over countless designs and wheel arrangements, many countries invariably going their own way in terms of design and policy. Until the 1920s many were conventional, British-styled designs, but the traditional 0-6-0s and 0-8-0s were unsuited to African conditions and instead often appeared in the form of 4-8-0s, 2-8-2s and 4-8-2s. As locomotives became larger, restrictions in axle weights, along with the tight curvatures, made the use of conventional locomotives increasingly difficult on many routes – until a design was conceived in Britain which was perfect for the African situation.

This revolutionary concept was H.W. Garratt's articulated design – the most important variation ever played on the conventional theme – which combined immense power with a light axle loading and the articulation required to negotiate the most tortuous curves. The Garratt's strength lay in the fact that the boiler was given its own separate frame and slung clear of all coupled wheels. Fuel and water were carried in separate units at either end, on which the boiler pivots were mounted. Thus, the double-jointed engine provided absolute freedom for the design of the boiler, firebox and ashpan, unimpeded by coupled wheels. The important question of weight distribution was solved by spreading the wheels either side of the boiler. Garratt persuaded the Manchester locomotive builder, Beyer Peacock, to adopt his principle and, from its inception in Edwardian Britain, it found favour in Africa.

The equipping of the Western world's railways with new forms of motive power and rolling stock created a whole range of industries keen to sell their products across all frontiers – and diesel salesmen regarded Africa as a rich hunting ground. The emotive appeal of investing in new technology is a great lure for Third World countries struggling to improve their lot. However, the use of sophisticated forms of motive power in the demanding conditions in Africa has often created problems, and many countries would have been far better served by relying on the steam locomotive's simplicity and longevity and concentrating such funds as were available upon improving track, rolling stock and communications, and investing in the right personnel.

Despite this, Africa still remains a haven for steam traction, but gone are the red-liveried, fire-throwing, eucalyptus-burning Garratts that worked the famous Benguela Railway of Angola. Gone also are the world's last Atlantics from Mozambique, but South Africa – for all its modernity – still sports a few main lines on which the 25 NC Class 4-8-4s, one of the world's largest steam survivors, remain.

Neighbouring Zimbabwe's railways have the distinction of being almost entirely Garratt-operated, a unique situation in which several classes provide a variety of services, such as passenger trains being hauled by the racy 15 Class 4-6-4 + 4-6-4s. Zimbabwe's adequate reserves of coal and her capacity to maintain steam traction ensures that change is not imminent; in 1989 the country was negotiating with South Africa for the purchase of a batch of 2S NC Class 4-8-4s.

Another African country that wisely realises the value of steam traction is Sudan. Here, massive problems have been encountered in maintaining complex and temperamental fleets of diesels, so a policy of partial reversion to steam was begun during the 1980s, greatly aided by Hugh Phillips Engineering of South Wales, the company responsible for renovating many of Sudan's locomotives. These played an important part in helping to alleviate the recent Sudanese famines and, as such, the liaison work undertaken by Hugh Phillips represents one of the bright spots on the world railway scene. After all, it is surely obligatory for Western nations to provide such simple and cheap spare parts to the developing world, instead of forcing upon them a technology that is often irrelevant to their situation.

On the former East African Railways Corporation, which comprised the combined networks of Kenya, Tanzania and Uganda, steam has sunk to a low ebb, although several classes do still see use in Tanzania. Sadly, the magnificent 59 Class 4-8-2 + 2-8-4 250-tonne Garratts, which formerly plied the 332-mile-long haul from Mombassa on the Indian Ocean up to the Kenyan capital of Nairobi, have now been replaced by diesels, but most of the class still exists out of use.

Compared with Africa, the Middle East has relatively few railways, although Egypt sports a well-engineered network which was once a perfect mirror of British practice and performance. Today, with the exception of isolated examples in Jordan, only Syria retains a small steam fleet on its curious Levantine gauge of 3ft 3⅝in. Radiating from Damascus, two principal routes are in operation: one heads through the mountains to the Lebanese border, while the other heads due south and was part of the original pilgrim route to Mecca. Trains work as far as Dar'a on the Jordanian border, where 2-8-0s and 2-8-2s of German origin are active. Other types lie abandoned at Cadem works in Damascus.

The last working survivor of the former East African Railway's 25 Class 2-8-2 (left) performs shunting duties around the yard at Tabora. She was built in Lancashire by the Vulcan Foundry in 1926 and looks completely at home alongside a typical British semaphore. The most spectacular line in the whole of East Africa was the 332-mile drag from Mombassa on the Indian Ocean up to the Kenyan capital, Nairobi. For many years, this was worked by the magnificent Mountain Class 4-8-2+2-8-4 Garratts (above). Named after the highest mountains of East Africa, thirty-four of these oil-burning giants were delivered to Kenya from Beyer Peacock's Gorton works, Manchester, in 1955. Overleaf: a brace of 16A Class 2-8-2+2-8-2 Garratts head along the West Nicholson to Bulawayo line in Rhodesia. The wagon sandwiched between the two locomotives serves to achieve a more even weight distribution on the track.

Although steam traction is rapidly declining on South Africa Railway's main lines, many historic classes can still be found in colliery service. Left: a former mainline 4-8-2 heads from the colliery to the exchange sidings with a loaded train, the workers riding on the engine. These magnificent 4-8-2 tanks – along with a 4-8-4 variant – can be seen at many South African industrial locations. The New Largo colliery has two 4-8-2s and a 4-8-4, all built by North British of Glasgow during the 1950s. 4-8-2 tanks have been used in South Africa since the 19th century and these engines are essentially a modern update of the earlier designs. The first example was built in 1937, and they are capable of starting 400-tonne trains on a one in fifty gradient. Above: one of New Largo's 4-8-2Ts, decked in its superb chocolate livery, draws empties from the adjacent power station sidings.

Left: the elegant Victorian lines of this ex South African Railways 7A Class 4-8-0 are clearly evidenced as she enjoys a further lease of life at the Whitbank Consolidated Coal Mine. She was built in 1886 at Sharp Stewart's Atlas Works, Glasgow, for the Cape Government Railway as a standard heavy freight design of the period. The practice of naming locomotives was adopted by various depots on South African Railways, especially at De Aar (bottom left), where many of the huge 25NC Class 4-8-4s took the names of their drivers' wives. Many hybridised locomotives exist on South Africa's industrial lines, the most common form being the 4-8-2Ts rebuilt into tender locomotives. These conversions are done locally, sometimes with bizarre results, but the example (below) at Tweefontein United Colliery in the Transvaal, has produced a colonial-looking 4-8-0. Many reasons are given for these conversions: leaking water from the tanks causing slipping, surging water in the tanks causing excess wear in the axle boxes, and even insufficient fuel-carrying capacity. In order to regain the lost adhesion, dummy splashes filled with cement or waste steel are set along the engine's running plate.

These pages: vintage steam operations along the route from Damascus to Lebanon. Friday is the Muslim day of rest, and special trains run to enable the inhabitants of Damascus to escape the searing heat of their traffic-choked city and spend a few hours of cool relief in the hills. The Lebanese civil war has long since prevented through workings on this line, and all trains terminate at Sergayah, on the Syrian side. Left: a Syrian 2-6-0T, built by SLM of Switzerland in 1894, prepares to return from Sergayah with an evening train to Damascus. Above: a heavily-laden Fridays-only excursion train climbs away from Damascus. Overleaf: as evening shadows lengthen, a Damascus-bound train leaves Sergayah behind an oil-burning Swiss-built 2-6-0T dating back to the 1890s.

The line southwards from Damascus was originally part of the pilgrim route to Mecca. Authorised by the Sultan of Turkey, building began in 1901, and seven laborious years later the line reached Medina, 809 miles to the south. But the Arabs, concerned that their Holy City would be defiled, refused to allow the railway any further and mounted frequent attacks on construction camps. Shortly afterwards, during World War I, sections of the line were destroyed by Lawrence of Arabia. Today, only the Syrian and part of the Jordanian sections remain operative. Facing page: a Hartmann-built 2-8-2 raises steam at Cadem depot in Damascus prior to taking a freight southwards to the Jordanian border. Above: the last survivor from a class of 2-8-0s provided by Hartmann of Chemnitz for the Hedjaz Railway heads the daily mixed along the pilgrim route from De Aar on the Jordanian border to Damascus and, returning later the same day (right), pauses to shunt at one of the many wayside stations. Overleaf: two of the Swiss-built 2-6-0Ts belonging to Syrian Railways raise steam at Sergayah prior to returning with passenger trains to Damascus.

STEAM IN SOUTH AMERICA

In common with Africa, South America is another vast region of the world comprised of countries which never built their own locomotives. Britain was the principle builder and supplier of railways to South America, not through Imperial rule, as had been the case in Africa, but through commercial and financial interests. South America's railways are among the most fascinating and varied on earth – here one experiences a multiplicity of countries and enormous geographical contrasts, ranging from the exotic trans-Andean routes, the jungles of the Amazon basin and the wilds of the Paraguayan Chaco to the fertile Argentinian pampas, the waterless deserts of Chile and the wildernesses of Patagonia.

South America is perhaps the last great steam hunting ground – just the place to discover an undocumented survivor. Modernisation has taken its toll, as have railway closures, which in some countries have been quite severe, but such isolated pockets as exist are eminently worthy of study. The exotica ranges from such delights as the world's last steam trams, American steam super power in the form of Texas type 2-10-4s, wood-burning Edwardian Moguls on the main line through Paraguay and the world's southernmost railway in Rio Gallegos, whose 2-10-2s haul 2,000-tonne coal trains.

At one time Argentina had the largest railway network on the continent – it is said the British built a greater mileage of railways there than they did at home. It was the British steam locomotive that opened up the vast, fertile pampas to become one of the bread baskets of the world, and in so doing, it made a significant contribution to one of South America's leading economies. British finance and engineering skills in this country were as predominant as they were in India and, not surprisingly, Argentina was the recipient of vast numbers of classic, homespun British locomotives, which for many years burnt coal imported from the Welsh valleys! Modernisations, closures and the general decline of railways has now ended this great chapter of railway history.

In neighbouring Brazil, steam survivors hail primarily from the United States. The country's best-loved system is the Dona Teresa Cristina, a metre gauge coal-carrying railway in the south. This last haunt of the Texas 2-10-4s also operates 2-10-2s purchased from Argentina's Belgrano Railway. Brazil's sugar plantations in the Campos and Pernambuco areas retain a remarkable diversity of American, British and German motive power on metre gauge networks, although many of the older designs are now out of use, joint victims of railway closures and dieselisation.

The situation in Paraguay is infinitely more exciting; here the world's last all-steam main line runs for 232 miles from the capital city of Asuncion to Encarnacion on the Argentinian border. Hardly anything has changed since the Edwardian engineers converted the line to standard gauge in 1910; some of the original Moguls remain operative, along with other British designs purchased in recent years from Argentina's Urquiza railway. The Paraguayan system, whose veteran wood-burning locomotives throw crimson embers a hundred feet into the air, is one of the highlights of the world steam scene. The workshops that maintain the system are set in the rural village of Sapucay and much of the machinery is steam powered, as was original nineteenth-century practice.

Uruguay has also been a major user of British Moguls since the early years of the century. The country's railways were financed and constructed by Britain and many of the engines came from Beyer Peacock's Gorton works. It seems likely that the Manchester connection with the Fray Bentos meat company was one of the reasons why that city provided so many of Uruguay's locomotives. The older Beyer Peacock survivors are the 2-6-0 tanks, some of which date back to the 1880s, but far more significant are the derelict examples of the world's last 4-4-4 suburban tanks. These graceful and beautifully proportioned machines are reminiscent of similar engines on the Wirral Railway and are the only surviving examples of this wheel arrangement – none exist in preservation. A massive investment in a road system has decimated Uruguay's railways and although isolated steam workings remain in several parts of the country, these are now confined to tripping and shunting duties.

Elsewhere, amid the vastness of South America, enclaves of steam traction survive, albeit often derelict, like the American classics dumped in the depot at Puerto Eten in Peru, such as a magnificent Rogers 4-4-0 complete with wooden cab – a definitive example of early American locomotive practice. Equally exotic rarities, like the last articulated Ritson Meyer 0-6-6-0s on the nitrate railways of Chile's Atacama Desert, have recently passed into history.

The magnificent British-built 4-8-0s were the principal freight haulers during the latter days of the Buenos Aires and Great Southern Railway. Facing page: one of a later batch delivered from the Vulcan Foundry in 1948, the year in which Argentina's railways were nationalised.

Argentina's former Buenos Aires and Great Southern Railway was almost entirely British financed, built and operated. It was one of the best-run railways in the world and its 5ft 6in inch gauge main lines opened up the fertile pampas and enabled the conveyance of inordinate tonnages of beef and grain to the Atlantic ports 'The BAGS', as the Railway was affectionately known, played a vital part in advancing Argentina's economy, making it one of the richest countries in the world. Such achievements are long since part of Argentina's history. Today, the unfashionableness of railways, combined with heavy dieselisation, has decimated former British designs. Facing page: a former BAGS 2-6-2T, built by Nasmyth Wilson at their Bridgewater foundry in Patricroft, Manchester, in 1907, eases a ballast train out of the sidings at Tandil. Above and right: a classic Scottish Pug in far flung Argentina, No. 2562 was the last survivor of a large class of 0-6-0 saddle tanks which formed a standard shunting design. She was built by Kerr Stuart of Stoke-upon-Trent in 1913, but the class originated from the North British of Glasgow in 1904 and bears all the hallmarks of a traditional Scottish 0-4-0 Pug developed during the middle years of the 19th century.

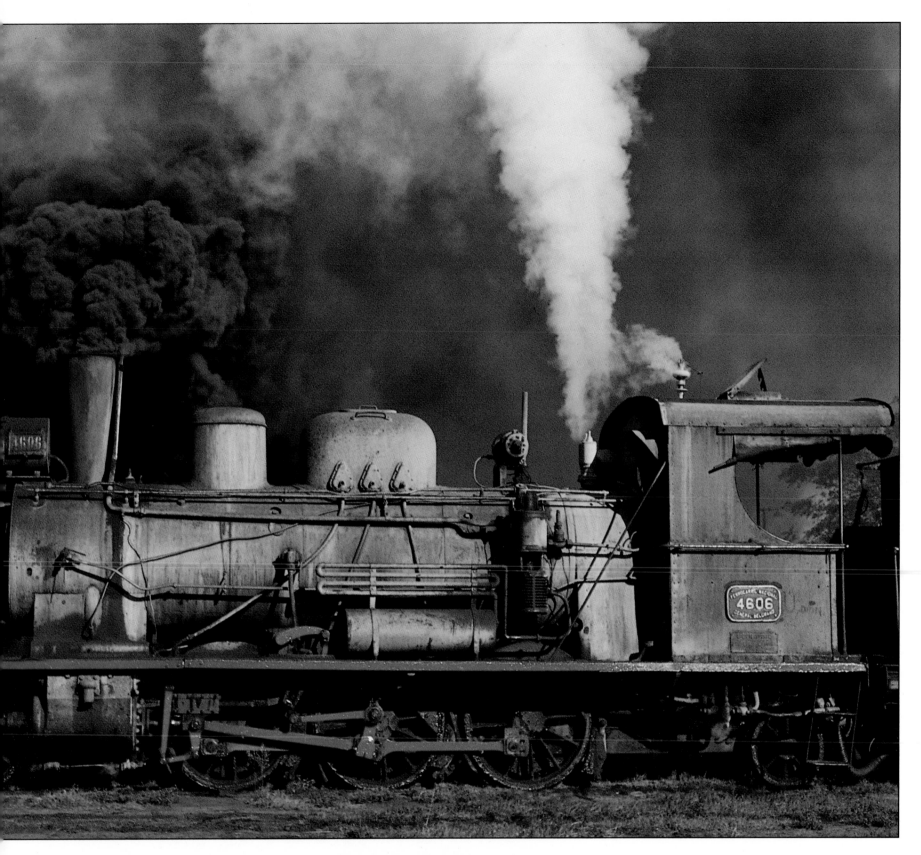

Top left: Argentina's metre-gauge Belgrano Railway Class 10A 2-6-2 No. 4606 heads away from Santa Fe with a pick-up freight. She was built by Société Suisse in 1909, during the time that the French owned the Santa Fe Railway. Earlier the same day, at the Sante Fe shed, No. 4606 (above) was summoned to cover for a failed diesel. Steam was raised hastily as heavy jets of oil were sprayed into the firebox. Soon her boiler pressure of 175 pounds was reached, and the seventy-year-old Swiss-built veteran was ready to tow the failed diesel back to the depot and take over the yard shunt. Left: a former Buenos Aires and Great Southern Railway 2-6-2 suburban tank ends its days as shed pilot at the Ingeniero White depot on the Atlantic coast. Introduced during the early years of the present century, these superb engines performed magnificently on the heavy suburban workings around Buenos Aires. Overleaf: one of Argentina's last surviving 15B Class 4-8-0s, No. 1583, built by the Vulcan Foundry in 1948, heads a heavy cement train along the Olavarria to Loma Negra line.

In the vastness of Brazil survive some of the world's most fascinating steam engines. The principal areas of steam activity are the sugar plantations of the Campos and, to a lesser extent, the Pernambuco regions further north. The diversity is indicated by the accompanying pictures, which show a British-built 4-4-0, 2-6-0 and 2-8-0. This lovely Mogul (bottom left) works for the Usina Santa Maria and is pictured far out in the plantations waiting for a rake of empty cane wagons to be filled. Notice her chimney top eaten away after years of fiery endeavour. She was one of a batch of Moguls delivered to the Leopoldina Railway from Beyer Peacock's works in Manchester during the 1890s. She was No. 204 and still bears the original plate on her cab side. Usina Santa Maria also sports this handsome 2-8-0 (left) which the Leopoldina Railway received from the North British of Glasgow in 1904. She is seen in the factory confines against piles of bagasse, which is used to fire the boilers of the mill. Below: one of Latin America's most delightful steam survivors is this handsome 4-4-0, which survives at Usina San Jose. As the works plate on her smokebox clearly reveals, she was built by Sharp Stuart's Atlas Works, Glasgow, in 1896.

Top left: a Uruguayan Railways B Class 2-6-0T built by Beyer Peacock in 1889 shunts the yards at Florida. She is coupled to a six-wheeled outside framed tender bearing Beyer Peacock plates. Left: the last survivor of Uruguayan Railways' T Class 2-8-0s, No. 139 'Ing Pedro Magnou', heads a mixed freight along the rickety, weed-strewn branch leading to the famous meat canning port of Fray Bentos, on the River Plate. The class once numbered eight locomotives, which were rebuilt in Uruguay from Hawthorn Leslie Moguls exported during the Edwardian period. Notice the brass nameplate, unusually situated on the side of the firebox. Above: the Dodo of the Atacama. The world's last surviving Kitson Meyer 0-6-6-0T heads a demolition train away from Taltal, on Chile's Pacific coast. The waterless Atacama Desert of Chile was the last refuge for the Kitson Meyer, which was an articulated predecessor of the more successful Garratt.

Above: the most modern engines on the Ferrocarril Presidente Carlos Antonio Lopez Railway in Paraguay are these Moguls, two of which were delivered from the Yorkshire Engine Company's Meadowhall works, Sheffield, in 1953. Shown is No. 152, *Asuncion*, with her nameplate set on the cab side. Right: *Don Carlos*, a 2-8-2 well tank, built by Manning Wardle of Leeds in 1916, at work on the Quebracho lines of the Paraguayan Chaco.

Above: the sad remains of the once-important running sheds at Location, on Ghana Railways. In the foreground is No. 181, a 4-6-0 built by Robert Stephenson, whilst inside the dismantled shed stand a pair of Beyer Peacock Pacifics in the process of being cut up. Overleaf: one of the largest of the locomotive mausoleums in Greece was at the old station in Thessalonika. The site contained around forty locomotives, including several types of great historical significance. Three are depicted here; in the foreground is one of the stately Austrian-designed 2-10-0s, behind which lie a number of Austrian 0-10-0s descended from Karl Golsdorf design, while rear left is one of the American-built S160s which came to Greece during World War II.

GRAVEYARDS AND SCRAPYARDS

A moribund locomotive exudes an atmosphere and presence which can be positively haunting. Lines of cold, inert engines waiting to be towed to breaker's yards are now a common sight across the world. Many will have little, if anything, mechanically wrong with them and this serves to make their situation even more poignant. Withdrawn locomotives can be found in three general locations. Firstly, there are those lying out of use at their depots, often standing alone or in small groups either at the back or at the side of the shed. Secondly, there are dumps of engines concentrated at a specific site – a 'graveyard' – usually well away from the sheds, and thirdly, there are examples actually inside scrapyards, where they are likely to remain for weeks, rather than months or years.

The distinction between a graveyard and scrapyard is enormous. In the former, the engines lie silently rusting, invariably accompanied by ever-encroaching vegetation. In tropical lands this can grow to enormous proportions as branches, trees and creepers liberally festoon the silent hulks. Wherever there is rusting metal, wild flowers seem to abound, and when these deck the engines in funereal purples, they provide a perfect background to the overriding mood of morbidity. Here the silence might be broken only by the soft, summery drone of bees – a dramatic contrast to the scrapyard, where the quiet humming of insects is replaced by the wrenching sounds of tearing metal and the bitter stench of acetylene gas. Breaking up a locomotive is a formidable task and one that is seldom done haphazardly. Even an example of modest size is worth a considerable sum of money, as there are many grades of metal, including non-ferrous items like copper fireboxes, which are always held at a premium.

The scrapyard is also a place of great flux; the piles of metal change almost daily, while in the graveyard, nothing changes, the shadows fall in predictable patterns, the plants and grasses flower and seed in their uninterrupted cycle and insects and birds proliferate.

The origin of a graveyard is often the consequence of indecision when, following the modernisation of a whole or part of a network, the locomotives are set aside, ostensibly as a reserve. Maybe they will be needed again one day in the event of a fuel crisis or a war? In other instances, it is a case of *manana* – a bureaucratic inability to agree a disposal price and method – and with scrap generally increasing in value, there is little incentive to reach speedy conclusions. In Scandinavia, Eastern Europe and Russia, some reserves are mothballed and the engines greased and boarded up, but these are exceptions – most of the world's dumps are left to go wild.

The ultimate dispatch of condemned locomotives takes many forms; sometimes they are cut up at the works of the owning railway and their parts cannibalised to keep other examples of the same type in service, or alternatively, they may be sold to contractors, who either come to the site and break the engines up or have them towed to their own yard. Where individual engines are concerned, the scrap contractor may well turn up with a lorry and several men and enact the job on the spot. A fascinating example of this occurred at a coalfield in Pathardi, Bengal, after a local scrapman had won the contract to break up a Beyer Peacock coalfield tank. He, along with eight of his men, turned up at the depot and pitched a tent in which they were all to live, and then they proceeded to demolish the hapless engine over the ensuing days with the aid of hammers! Where larger concentrations of engines are concerned, however, it is usually considered expedient to convey them to a scrapyard.

Some graveyards have achieved considerable fame; those in Greece, for example, were highly distinctive. Some of the sites were fifteen years old when they were finally closed and contained veterans ranging from Austro-Hungarian designs through to American types delivered as part of U.S aid to the allies during World War II.

In Britain, apart from closed depots which contained withdrawn engines pending ultimate disposal, the steam locomotive disappeared very quickly – but for the single exception of Woodham's yard in Barry, South Wales. This scrapyard, which eventually turned into a huge graveyard, originally took over 200 locomotives from British Railways during the early 1960s. Hardly any were broken up and their retention provided a vast repository for preservationists, who had time to build up funds to buy particular engines, having put a reserve on the items of their choice. Dozens of locomotives were subsequently rescued from Woodham's yard in this way, including many of those currently seen hauling specials over British Rail's main lines, and today, some thirty years after the first examples were consigned to Barry, the last handful are being rescued. This yard belies the glorious suggestion that hundreds of British locomotives have been stored in abandoned tunnels as part of a strategic reserve – a tale which occurs, with varying degrees of credibility, every few years.

Yet in the world at large, little basis for preservation exists and the half-forgotten lines of sad hulks which remain will eventually vanish into oblivion. Nevertheless, one can hope that a few unsung little workhorses now languishing in the undergrowth will one day be reclaimed by future generations as silent witnesses to the greatest of the railway's legends.

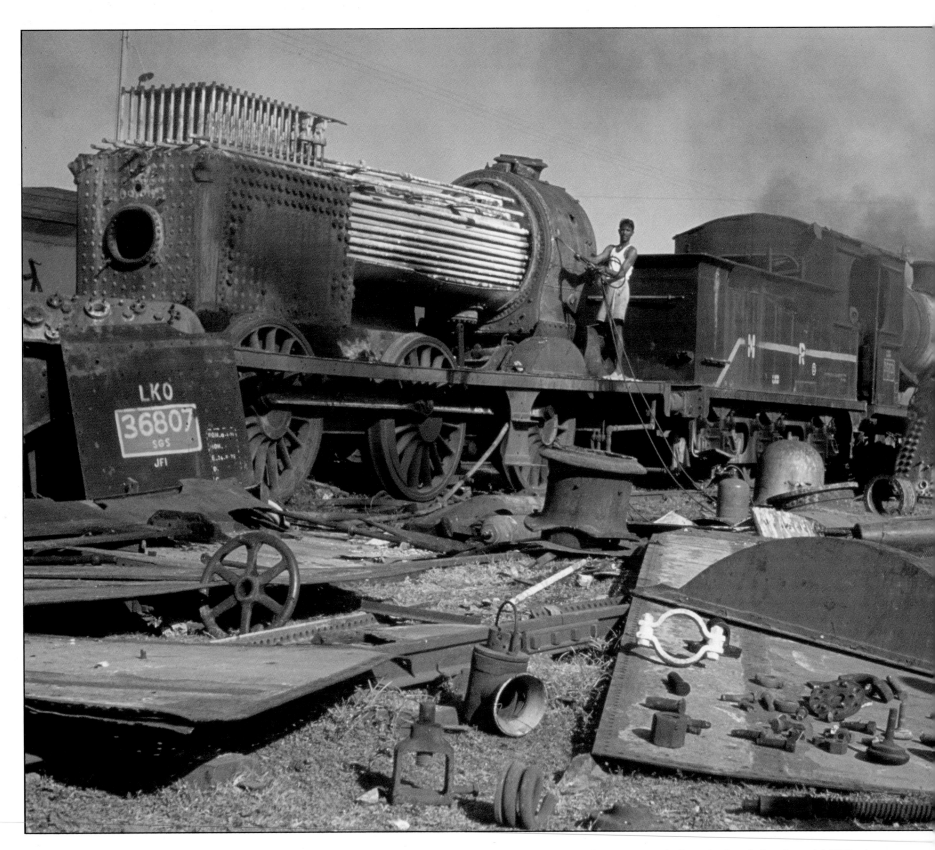

Above: this scene in the breaker's yard at Sultanpur, in Northern India, during the mid 1970s shows the mass breaking up of former British types which took place during that period A line of inside cylinder 0-6-0s dating back to the BESA years is seen on the left, alongside a boiler from one of the XA Class light Pacifics from the X series standards of the 1920s and '30s. The cab side of the left-hand engine indicates that she was an SGS Class, whilst the LKO is an abbreviation for Lucknow, the engine's last home depot. She was built at Armstrong Whitworth's legendary works on the Scotswood Road in Newcastle-upon-Tyne in 1923. Right: a piston lies forlornly against pieces of abandoned anatomy on the floor of the breaker's yard.

Left: another scene at Sultanpur, as the boiler of an SGS Class inside cylinder 0-6-0 is cut open, revealing the tubes coloured white from scale. The dome cover has fallen to the ground, as has the lamp from the buffer beam, whilst the pile of flaming oil rags in the foreground is used to ignite the acetylene torch. Above: the wheel has come full circle for this mighty XE Class Mikado 2-8-2 built on the Clyde by William Beardmore of Dalmuir in 1930. For almost half a century these giants hauled 2,000-tonne coal trains over the hill regions of Bengal. They were the most powerful conventional locomotives to work on Indian Railways and a total of ninety-three were put into traffic between their inception in 1928 and 1945, when the final batch was delivered. The earlier BESA type 2-8-0 in the background emphasises the XE's mighty proportions. Notice the pieces of anatomy in the foreground: a piston, crank axle, dome cover, chimney, valves, springs, wheel fragments and a buffer.

Above: a tale of two engines. Sudan Railway's 500 Class No. 514 resembles the carcass of a dead animal as it lies alongside the Rabak to Knana line following a derailment many years ago. In the background, sister engine No. 541 approaches with a mixed train. The 500 Class are Sudan's most powerful freight locomotives and were delivered to the Sudan in the form of aid from the North British works of Glasgow during the 1950s. By 1983, when this picture was taken, a serious shortage of spare parts had led to only three members of the class remaining in service, despite the fact that they were needed and were preferable in Sudanese conditions to the temperamental and complex nature of diesel locomotives. The situation is a little better today, with Britain somewhat belatedly assisting with the supply of spares, both for the 500 Class and other types of locomotive in the Sudan. Right: the wreck of *Khor Doniya*, a Sudan Railways Pacific No. 245 built by North British, lies at the bottom of a bank on the lightly laid section between Sennar and Damazeen. The disaster occurred during a night of exceptionally heavy rain, which caused the embankment to give way. The engine is irretrievable and destined to lie in that remote spot for all time, as the Damazeen section is too lightly laid to permit a sufficiently heavy crane to facilitate a rescue.

Left: the atmosphere of the locomotive graveyard is epitomised in this scene from Cadem works, Damascus, showing the remains of a Hartmann-built 2-8-0 dating back to the early years of the present century. Above: the 0-4-2 was one of the earliest forms of passenger locomotive; it evolved during the 1830s and had all but vanished by the early decades of the 20th century. Accordingly, the discovery of this hulk in Java during the 1970s was of tremendous significance. Of typical Beyer Peacock design, she was delivered to Java during the 1880s for the island's standard-gauge network, although nothing had operated on this gauge since 1942, when the Japanese invaded Java and looted all the standard-gauge equipment for shipment to Manchuria. And so this amazing survivor was left abandoned in the jungle for the following thirty-five years.

Left: the Polish State Railways 600mm gauge PX27 Class 0-8-0T No. 775 lies abandoned near Wenecja. Above: the scene in the Feldbahn graveyard at Czarna Bialostocka, featuring Feldbahn TX Class No. 232 built by Henschel in 1916 for operations during World War I.

Above: the Insular Lumber Company's incredible 0-6-6-0 four-cylinder compound Mallet lies abandoned following the cessation of logging operations. The haunted atmosphere which always surrounded this engine during its chequered career remains in full evidence despite its moribund state. Right: this 0-4-2 side tank lying abandoned on the privately owned Rejo Agung sugar plantation in Java is one of the island's rarest locomotives. She came from the little-known Dickson Manufacturing Company of Scranton, Pennsylvania, whose last locomotive was turned out in 1909 and the example seen here is one of five which the company sent to Java in 1900.

Left: the wreck of *Tithorea*, one of the stately Austrian Class 580 2-10-0s which until the 1960s hauled heavy passenger trains over the main line from Athens to Thessalonika. Following an accident many years ago, this example was pushed into a line-side coppice and abandoned.

Above: Britain's first 2-10-0s were built for military operations during World War II. All came from the North British of Glasgow and, in common with other designs for wartime, saw service over a wide area. Sixteen were ceded to Greece after the war, and these examples survived long after their sisters had vanished from other countries. Their light axle loading rendered them suitable for a wide variety of routes, particularly in the north, on the main line leading to the Turkish border. Classified Lb by the Greek State Railways, three of the class are depicted here in the locomotive graveyard at Thessalonika. Overleaf: another scene from the Thessalonika graveyard in northern Greece, depicting one of the Austrian 580 Class 2-10-0s. Classified La by the Greek State Railways, this engine was built for Greece in 1927 by Skoda of Czechoslovakia.

233

Above: the end of the steam age in Ghana as British built locomotives lie abandoned at Location works. Facing the camera is Hunslet 0-8-0T, flanked on the left by a Beyer Peacock Pacific, and on the right by a Vulcan Foundry 4-8-2. Right and above right: further examples of Britain's engineering prowess amid the locomotives and machine tools at Location works. The building of Ghana Railways over the uncharted, swamp-infested, malaria-riddled interior of the Gold Coast is a typical example of Britain's legendary pioneering of railways across the world. Overleaf: out to grass. The abandonment of railway operations on the sugar plantations around Tebicuary, in Paraguay, rendered these metre-gauge veterans redundant. An Orenstein and Koppel 0-4-0 well tank (left) reposes alongside Baby Chaco, an 0-6-0 of 1898 with Stephenson link motion. Last page: in her heyday, this lovely 4-4-0 worked elegant passenger trains over Brazil's metre-gauge Mogiana Railway and was one of a class exported to Brazil from Sharp Stewart's works in Glasgow during the 1890s. Compare this sad hulk with one of her sister engines depicted in full working glory on page 211.